Chakras

Practical Meditation Guides for Reaching Balance in Real Life

(A Guide to Chakra Healing Balance Chakras Improve Your Health and Feel Great)

Stephen Barry

Published By **Jordan Levy**

Stephen Barry

All Rights Reserved

Chakras: Practical Meditation Guides for Reaching Balance in Real Life (A Guide to Chakra Healing Balance Chakras Improve Your Health and Feel Great)

ISBN 978-1-7770663-6-9

No part of this guidebook shall be reproduced in any form without permission in writing from the publisher except in the case of brief quotations embodied in critical articles or reviews.

Legal & Disclaimer

The information contained in this book is not designed to replace or take the place of any form of medicine or professional medical advice. The information in this book has been provided for educational & entertainment purposes only.

The information contained in this book has been compiled from sources deemed reliable, and it is accurate to the best of the Author's knowledge; however, the Author cannot guarantee its accuracy and validity and cannot be held liable for any errors or omissions. Changes are periodically made to this book. You must consult your doctor or get professional medical advice before using any of the suggested remedies, techniques, or information in this book.

Upon using the information contained in this book, you agree to hold harmless the Author from and against any damages, costs, and expenses, including any legal fees potentially resulting from the application of any of the information provided by this guide. This disclaimer applies to any damages or injury caused by the use and application, whether directly or indirectly, of any advice or information presented, whether for breach of contract, tort, negligence, personal injury, criminal intent, or under any other cause of action.

You agree to accept all risks of using the information presented inside this book. You need to consult a professional medical practitioner in order to ensure you are both able and healthy enough to participate in this program.

Table Of Contents

Chapter 1: What Is Meditation?............... 1

Chapter 2: The Power Of Crystals 23

Chapter 3: What Is A Chakra? 46

Chapter 4: What Is Energy?..................... 61

Chapter 5: The Benefits Of An Alkaline Diet 88

Chapter 6: What Are Chakras?............. 120

Chapter 7: The Seven Foremost Chakras 167

Chapter 8: Balancing And Recuperation Your Chakras... 181

Chapter 1: What Is Meditation?

Before jumping right into all of the statistics approximately meditation, I'll begin with the aid of manner of telling you what meditation is. Meditation is the exercise of being aware, calming your thoughts, and focusing your interest for your breath. You do not want to block out the feelings or the thoughts that input your mind however alternatively get hold of them and allow them to pass. You may also listen noises on the identical time as meditating, word them then release them. Meditation ought to not be a chore; as an possibility, its miles a way to preserve your mind smooth of muddle.

The exercise of meditation has been round for lots of years. Anyone can discover ways to meditate, however it does take exercising. Do no longer get irritated if you can't sit down despite the fact that or interest to your breath for a difficult and rapid amount of time. Set a to be had aim. There are a few apps available in which you could start for two minutes, and that they assist you be successful. There are many strategies to meditate; concentrating in your breath, guided meditations, and chanting are just a few of them.

Many human beings acquire as authentic with mindfulness and meditations are the equal; at the same time as they will be comparable, they may be high-quality. Meditating is even as you attention on your breath and produce your attention indoors of yourself. Mindfulness is in which you have a have a look at matters no judgmentally. Meditation is commonly executed in a seated function or mendacity down. Mindfulness allows to boom attention. Mindfulness can be finished everywhere, together with while on foot or doing dishes. One exciting issue approximately mindfulness is you discover ways to obtain a few issue without judgment; you no longer see topics as black and white or unique or horrible.

There are many forms of meditation:

Loving-kindness meditation is to help you release horrible feelings and promote kindness and empathy.

A frame take a look at is like it sounds, you experiment your body, and be privy to it in detail. Release stress at the same time as you find tension in advantageous regions.

Mindfulness meditation is at the same time as you stay inside the gift 2nd and study topics round you without judgment.

Breath meditation is wherein you recognition to your breath and turn your thoughts inward.

These are just a few examples of all of the remarkable meditations that can be completed.

Where Should You Meditate?

The awesome area to meditate is anywhere you revel in comfortable. There are some locations more perfect than others. Typically you need quiet vicinity and now not using distractions, in particular at the same time as you're a amateur. Some humans tell you which you want to have a particular room to meditate in; this is not the case. Each parents has an area in which we experience the maximum snug. That is the area I must advise.

Here is some useful data whilst searching out the best location to meditate. Some people want to meditate by means of way of drawing their curtains, so there isn't as an lousy lot slight. Others want to sit down out of doors within the solar, in which they're able to enjoy the warmth on their face. The remarkable location to meditate is in that you revel in the maximum cushty, can track into your breath, and recognition on yourself.

There are many strategies to situate yourself for meditation; the key's to get cushty for YOU. It can be repute, laying down flat on the floor, sitting, lying in mattress, strolling, or maybe strolling out. It's quite masses placing your thoughts in an altered kingdom. My cousin has hassle meditating, however even as he's shadow boxing or sparring, he is in the best country of mind.

The majority of humans have a hard time finding time to meditate. Our lives are so busy; we rush to work, run domestic, make dinner, and try to match in family time too. It can seem not viable to locate five extra minutes in the day to take time to meditate.

One way to make time is to set a timer, although it's most effective for 5 mins, and meditate.

Another place you may meditate is with organizations. When I first observed to meditate, I started out with organization meditation. About ten people may visit a studio that the owner set up for rest sports. It became an fantastic manner to learn. You get the advantages of meditation. You moreover had been with individuals who shared a commonplace interest.

Once you find out your location to meditate, what's your subsequent step? Some human beings selected to stare upon an item and focus their interest on it. Others choose out to take a seat with their eyes closed. You can attempt every processes to appearance which one you need. When you're organized, begin gently breathing in and out, focusing on the air going into your lungs after which liberating it. When your mind starts offevolved to wander, it will just lightly bring it lower decrease lower back in your breath.

Why Should You Meditate?

There are many reasons to begin meditating. Meditation will help you turn out to be greater attuned alongside aspect your frame and your emotions. I began out meditating due to the fact I grow to be aggravating, normally on aspect, and took the whole thing in my view. When I begin to enjoy that way now, I take some breaths, pay attention completely on my breath, and, at the same time as feasible, near my eyes. Doing those steps allows me to find out my middle and get keep of what I'm feeling. I attention on my internal goodness, and it permits to look the larger photo. An exciting thing I've been suggested is Meditation can help prevent binge ingesting. Being aware about the purpose you're consuming lets in you understand in case you're hungry or not.

During the day, we often are misplaced in belief. We aren't specializing in what we are doing, our minds are wandering, and we are busy searching across the room in region of that specialize in what we need to be doing. While meditation won't help you multitask, it'll assist keep you focused and higher able to stay on challenge. At artwork, most humans have a couple of obligation. When you are going for walks on one trouble, then every different technique takes priority. Meditation makes it less complicated to shift your recognition a few of the 2 duties.

Meditation lets you sleep higher. I maintain in thoughts that maximum people should use help getting a better night time time's sleep. When you get extra sleep, you clearly feel higher. Getting good enough sleep has been established to help beautify your immune tool and enhance your reminiscence and mood. In addition to assisting you sleep higher, meditation moreover decreases your anxiety. One symptom of anxiety is racing thoughts. Meditation permits to sluggish down racing thoughts and shift your reputation to your self and your breath.

Who Should Meditate?

In the remaining ten years or so, human beings have started out transferring their interest to intellectual health. Once the focus began to transport, the blessings of meditation became greater glaring. Now we apprehend that meditation can advantage almost everyone. If intellectual health is neglected at some stage in lifestyles, then like bodily fitness, it takes time to capture up. Anyone who wishes a manner to reduce strain and enhance self-cognizance want to take in meditating. In my private evaluations I actually have observed out that individuals who address Depression, Aniexty, Stress, Angermanagement, Addiction and considered one of a type intellectual fitness troubles benefit significantly from meditation.

Some humans count on excellent a pick out few can meditate that they may't meditate because they're capable of't prevent questioning or can't popularity on their breath. It can seem intimidating while you take a look at about people who have to meditate for lengthy durations while you remember that they started. It took me a 12 months in advance than I become capable of meditate for more than ten mins correctly. Most people have plenty of pressure in our lives, and our brains continuously recollect what we want to do. It makes experience we have were given trouble calming our minds; practice can be the splendid manner to overcome that hurdle.

Some people get their electricity by using way of being on my own, known as introverts, and a few humans get strength by way of using being round people; those are extroverts. While every of these kinds advantage from meditation, the introvert also can advantage extra. Typically introverts stay of their head, believing that they'll be self-aware. Instead, they overthink the whole thing, which harms them. Meditation can remind you to sluggish down, focus on your self, and turn out to be greater self-conscious.

Extroverts get their strength with the resource of being around humans, making experience they may have a greater hard time getting to know to meditate. Some grow to be so irritated in advance than even beginning believing they'll never do it that they in no way even start. Mistakenly believing they must sit down however for 5-10 minutes from the start, reality be informed, they will by no means get to ten mins. Start small, set a reason of 1 minute, and be thrilled with your self at the same time as you acquire it. Suppose you could in no way upward push up to greater than 5 minutes, then that's 5 more minutes than you used to do.

We understand how tough it is able to be to address essential social interactions for those who revel in social tension, from the intrusive mind of what if's to the awkwardness of creating small communicate. When you actively attempt to push the thoughts away, they pass decrease again with renewed stress, making the anxiety worse. Meditation indicates us a way to pay interest within the period in-between and now not to decide what we are feeling. Meditation does now not give up at the equal time as you are completed meditating however is a workout you could take with you. Instead of residing on the belief, have a have a examine it, apprehend it and launch it. When you are actively inside the second, it's going to help you hobby at the alternative character and concentrate to them at the equal time as taking the focus off your self.

What Are The Benefits of Meditation?

There are so many blessings of meditation; you may likely write a e-book based totally on that by myself. The maximum obvious of the benefits is studying to clear your mind on the equal time as focusing to your breath. Learning to smooth your thoughts and shift your reputation can be the maximum difficult part of learning to meditate. Also "Raising you frequency" or vibration which essentially approach shifting your intellectual country of consciousness.

Meditation improves your intellectual fitness: One of the pleasant subjects approximately meditation is its capability to reduce strain, anxiety and depression. Meditation lets in to build capabilities that alternate the way you react to annoying conditions. How does it do that? Some humans who've chronic stress or tension problems are often in combat or flight mode. This is a normal strain reaction for human beings in risky situations. When your frame is regularly inside the flight or fight response, it places a pressure in your coronary coronary coronary heart and splendid physical organs. Meditation allows fight the ones results via supporting you take a look at new procedures to manipulate strain which we will communicate more approximately in financial disaster 6 & 7. Meditation can help enhance creativity. This blessings you in worrying situations as it offers you an outlet. About a 12 months inside the beyond I began out portray. I am in no way a great painter, but I enjoy it, and it's a few problem that facilitates me lighten up.

Meditation helps you to reputation on the triumphing and permit drift of negative thoughts. It furthermore permits us to have a have a look at our thoughts with out judgment and then release them. Anxiety is at the same time as you worry approximately some thing that would by no means arise. We all worry needlessly. Meditation won't prevent you from worrying, but it'll assist you apprehend when you are doing it and refocus your mind on some factor else. Sadly part of being human is terrible thoughts; frequently, those mind are focused on ourselves. When you get unique at mediation, you could discover ways to separate your real mind from those subconsciously picked up. "Jim Kwik," the writer of infinite, talks approximately the internal talk, for all the ones thoughts won't be yours.

One neat aspect is that present day research have tested that meditation bodily adjustments the thoughts. According to a bit of writing in Psychology Today (Ahamod, Samoon MD, 2019), Mediation has been examined to trade many components of the brain, together with the left hippocampus, and this causes a reduction of gray matter range which controls interest. The regions of the mind that the changes have an effect on impacts cognitive ability, which include reminiscence and emotional law. Studies have observed thoughts changes after eight weeks of meditating. If without a doubt eight weeks can also have such an large impact in your thoughts, consider what eight years can do.

People with Attention Deficit Hyperactivity Disorder (ADHD) have a couple of problems with interest, together with impulse manipulate, sitting nevertheless, focusing, talking, plus others. For example, whilst my friend's son have come to be in kindergarten, that that they had a color chart for children who misbehaved. Due to his lack of potential to sit down nonetheless, the instructor made a new shade for him. It become not because he misbehaved; it come to be because of his disability to take a seat nonetheless. An-precise thing of ADHD is trouble drowsing. My pal did not recall it as meditation at the time, but at night time time, she would possibly positioned on moderate jazz, classical, or 70's soul track, all of which can be utilized in meditation, and had him close his eyes and be aware of it. It worked, he modified into capable of fall asleep quicker, and a few other gain is he though likes jazz.

What is your preferred sort of song? People with ADHD have a extra tough time meditating due to their brains constantly going and their difficulty sitting nonetheless. The purpose of meditation is to calm the mind, not stop the frame from transferring. As the mind relaxes, the body will take a look at. Once you may gradual down the body, discover a cushty function. Some will will let you realize not to get too snug, in any other case you'll fall asleep. If you fall asleep whilst meditating, then you definately want sleep.

Heart illness and strokes are of the most com-mon processes human beings die. An risky weight loss plan is one of the most extraordinary factors determining if you may get heart sickness. Another vital issue is strain and the way you control it. Long-term pressure does no longer in reality cause intellectual problems but bodily ones too. We understand that meditation can decrease your pressure level and assist you find out more wholesome strategies to deal with it.

Meditation enables to create extra kindness for your existence. Acceptance happens due to the fact you're studying to have greater compassion for your self and others. Releasing judgment takes area due to the fact you shape the potential to allow your mind come, have a look at them, and then launch them without judgment inside the path of meditation. The act of empathy is while you can recognize the way another feels. This takes place with meditation because of allowing your self to enjoy your feelings in preference to pushing them down. Learning those new competencies will enhance your relationships with the ones round you.

Empathy won't be the primary purpose of meditation, even though it helps us come to be extra compassionate, kind, and empathetic inside the route of others. An article pub-lished on September 29, 2012, within the Oxford Academic confirmed even in quick-term mediation beginners training, there was a effective impact on compassionate feelings for others. This might be due to the reduced quantities of pressure and tension humans skilled because of every day meditation. Interestingly sufficient, mind scans furthermore confirmed that those who meditate additionally have prolonged mind hobby inside the thoughts area linked with empathy. Another cause that it is able to increase empathy is that we have have been given distanced ourselves from one an-one-of-a-type due to the internet and absence of face-to-face in-teraction.

While spending time in the clinical area as a Drug and Alcohol abuse counselor and EMT,

I observed this primary hand. I determined that normally, one of the motives for drug abuse modified into to help relieve pain. There are un-derlying emotional motives that people begin the utilization of medicine or alcohol. Meditation has been able to help human beings in overcoming dependancy and handling the triggers. While meditation can not update reha-bilitation or walking a software, it's miles an first rate tool similarly to this system. Meditation teaches healthy coping strategies which the addict can use at the identical time as managing temptation. People have a propensity to use alcohol and drugs as a way to control while annoying situations. Needing to find new ways to manage is mainly re-quired while attending to their new life with out capsules. The exercising of meditation allows them to realize awful belief styles that would result in relapse.

Studies have verified that meditation enables to decrease ache thru 40%. Even when the man or woman emerge as meditat-ing, their ache have become no longer as excessive as those who have been not. As we mentioned earlier, meditation has been shown to change the mind. Meditation has been located to assist the pain related to chronic conditions which incorporates again pain, irritable bowel syndrome (IBS), and headaches. The key to the blessings is to hold to meditate; otherwise, the ache returns to the intensity it changed into at previously. The fantastic statistics for the ones new to meditation is it's going to also help them.

Blood strain measures the quantity of strain that is needed to deliver blood inside the course of your body. Age, consuming behavior, salt intake, and special factors affect blood stress and the amount of stress it takes to pump blood in the course of your frame. It has been proven that meditation can decrease blood stress for human beings who've borderline excessive blood stress.

Scientists bear in mind one motive it's miles beneficial is meditation helps you to create and hold healthy conduct. Meditation can't replace treatment, but it could take the place of a 2nd remedy.

Chapter 2: The Power Of Crystals

Crystals had been round for hundreds of years. There had been references to crystals as early as biblical times; they have been used for decorative and healing capabilities. Crystals are used for transmutation of strength in the body due to the reality the houses of the have an effect on our very very own energetically. In historic Greece, humans used crystals for safety and to thrust back evil spirits. Alchemists used a mixture of herbs and crystals to make healing remedies for the ill or injured. As time moved on, the advantages of crystals have come to be widely identified and more famous.

Crystals assist to heal due to the fact they absorb restoration electricity while freeing terrible energy. Some believe that the horrific energy goes into the earth to be reformed as high excellent energy. After the alternate of power, the character will experience non violent and characteristic greater energy.

Crystals are made of obviously formed factors from round the vicinity. Many gemstones are shaped with the useful resource of exposure to a few factor that emits immoderate heat. Amethyst is a crystal that paperwork whilst uncovered to lava. As they set within the moonlight, nature, and the sun, they believe that they benefit powerful recuperation energies. This is the strength that we all have access to and why they are able to purify the energy we already have.

There isn't any rule at the right way to apply crystals. Many people placed on them as rings. When sporting crystals as jewelry, they feel proper toward your pores and pores and skin; on occasion, there may be a coolness to it that slowly will become greater comforting because it warms up. Because of the enjoyable feeling you get from carrying the crystal, you lighten up sufficient to allow for energetic alignment.

Some human beings want to feature crystals to their water bottles. I even have additionally seen bottles made with crystals already in them. Many remember that including crystals to the water reasons the water to cope with its residences. Another well-known manner to function crystals to your lifestyles is to have them on the backs of chairs or areas in your property. I actually have person crystals in each room of my residence. What crystals you use will rely upon what room you're walking on and what you want to do with that room. An instance of this, want restoration light? Put selenite and citrine in a bowl on the window seal.

You can positioned crystals beneath your pillow even as you sleep to help you get a restful night time's sleep. A friend of mine turn out to be going through a whole lot of troubles and couldn't sleep. I gave her selenite to assist calm her and help her sleep. She endorsed me that it labored wonders. Many years later, she although sleeps with it via her bed.

No crystals are alike, and neither are their vibrations. One stone that could enjoy remarkable to one person will now not have an effect on each distinct. That's why while you purchase a modern day crystal; you want to preserve it and experience it earlier than you purchase it. Take a while to handle it. Do you experience a connection to it? How does it experience on your palm? Do you revel in a tingle, vibration, or every distinct sensation? What do you revel in about the crystal? Close your eyes and attention on it.

The second step to finding the appropriate crystal is why do you want to apply the crystal? Is it for precise fortune, healing, love, and releasing negativity? Each crystal has specific attributes that help with a desire of things. Amethyst allows alleviate guilt, rose quartz attracts love and peace, citrine for creativity, and green Aventurine for proper fortune. This is only a small list of what extraordinary stones can do.

One exciting problem to recognise is without a doubt because of the reality a crystal works one way for one man or woman, that doesn't suggest it will art work the same way for some other. Like you could sense the vibrations of the crystals, it is able to moreover revel in yours. If you make a decision to purchase a crystal for a person, don't be surprised within the occasion that they do now not discover it impossible to resist as lots as you do.

In the previous couple of years, mother and father have started out the usage of baltic amber necklaces for their youngsters in some unspecified time in the future of teething to relieve the ache. This works because of the fact the necklace might be cool within the mouth, and that allows alleviate the ache. Another motive is when a infant is teething, chewing on a few factor allows the tooth come through, lowering the ache. Amber has a assets that motives drooling to growth, which reduces inflammation. When the swelling within the gums is going down, the ache moreover does.

A new big use for gems is what's called a gemstone rubdown. This is a rub down that includes the use of gems. Adding the crystals offers the recipient the restoration blessings of the gemstones getting used. The rocks aren't used at a few level inside the complete rubdown however as an opportunity on some body elements that want extra healing. In addition to the gems, rubdown wands also are used. The rub down therapist will ask you inquiries to choose out what crystals will work notable for you. Like crystals and stones for restoration, getting a massage with crystals may want to have some of the equal blessings.

Tuning Forks

Initially, musicians used tuning forks to help tune their gadgets. Many years later, physicians positioned that they will use them to discover wherein listening to loss have come to be coming from. By the 1800s, humans have been the usage of these to experiment with how specific tones resonated with numerous people. As scientists did more research over time, they decided that tuning forks need to balance and heal the body.

The concept within the back of the use of tuning forks is that all subjects vibrate at precise frequencies, on the aspect of our power, muscle businesses, tissues, brain, organs, and bones. There are other techniques to apply tuning forks to heal. You can each use them for vibration recovery or sound treatment healing. When the usage of them for sound recuperation, you alter the tuning fork's sound until the frequency suits the restoration place.

Like acupuncture, in which needles are used to release stagnant strength, tuning forks artwork the identical way. The distinction between acupuncture and tuning forks, aside from the needles, is tuning forks use sound and vibration to reason recovery. You can use tuning forks for your body via placing the stem on precise pressure elements and allowing vibration to go with the flow via.

Tuning forks are to be had in a single-of-a-kind sizes, weights, and diverse sound frequencies referred to as Hz. Unweighted tuning forks offer off a valid it's much less hard to concentrate than weighted ones. You activate the tuning department by way of the usage of the use of a rubber p.C. Or some mallet to hit it, after which you'll be privy to the sound.

There are a few special techniques you could use a tuning fork for ache comfort. One of the strategies uses an unweighted tuning fork. The unweighted ones have a far clearer sound than weighted ones. In this approach, you don't touch the body however are actually above it and slowly pass to and fro over it. If the sound quits, faucet the fork another time to have the sound start yet again.

Another method is the use of two weighted tuning forks. We will use those forks at once at the body. Having it proper now on the body allows to goal a specific area specially. If the tuning fork motives the individual ache, you could located some factor at the surrender of it. The very last approach I'm going to tell you approximately is weighted tuning forks. These received't touch the body, but they will be close to enough to have an effect on the painful location. One of the strategies I use the tuning fork with the 432Hz and the omm 136.1 is keeping them over my electricity facilities and feeling the effects.

I actually have a One Year vintage infant woman named Luna Reign who loves gambling with the tuning forks. It's one in each of her desired things to do, and on every occasion it jewelry she smiles the most vital smile.

There are many advantages to the use of tuning forks. Below you can find out some of them:

Aids digestion

Balances the fearful tool

restores the frame to its herbal rhythm

Natural, anti inflammatory

Better sleep

Relaxes muscle tension

keeps anxiety and stresses doable

balances your frame's Ph,

permits to alleviate ache

relaxes anxiety in the muscle tissue

These are all benefits of the usage of vibrational treatment.

Incense

Incense has been used thinking about the truth that the start of time. They had been used as religious services, purification rituals, and open up minds for spiritual studies. It is assumed that the usage of incense can put off negativity from your property.

Incense is made from herbs and flowers, just so they provide off such a pleasing fragrance on the same time as burnt. Many humans burn incense due to the perfume on my own. Its aroma reduces stress, brings a experience of calm and a experience of peace. The fragrance can assist cowl up odors within the home, on the side of a weight room or a litter field.

There are many specific kinds of incense, such as cones, sticks, coils, and powder. No matter huge variety which fashion you pick out, they all have the identical advantages. The crucial difference among every kind is how they burn.

Cones have a pleasing decorative appearance due to the fact they normally have a pleasing-searching base which you set the cone on, and it gives off a float of smoke.

Sticks you area in an incense holder, and the smoke flows off, leaving ash to drop into the incense holder.

Coils incense are for folks that want the fragrance to final for a extra extended quantity of time. This form of incense can burn up to 2 hours.

Powder incense is fabricated from numerous scents burnt over charcoal in a bowl, plate, or a few aspect similar. There also are specific bowl packing containers you may use.

There are many blessings to the use of incense:

Clear Negative Energy

There are many strategies to easy negativity from your property, the most not unusual being sage. You can similarly use incense. You light the incense as you normally may. The smoke from the incense will smooth the power whilst you place your purpose to the room. Make pleasant you get the corners and doors actual.

Connect To Your Memories

Most human beings have reminiscences approximately the beyond which may be brought on with the useful resource of a fragrance. Incense will will let you connect to recollections and experience them all yet again. Dial cleansing cleaning soap always makes me do not forget going camping.

To Help You Relax And Unwind

Some scents cause humans to sense clearly cushty. This is a benefit acquired from burning incense. It can help muscle tissue to loosen and launch tension. At the save you of an prolonged worrying day, there's no longer something better than a pleasant heat bath with candles and incense eliminating a chilled aroma. The smoke's calming perfume can assist slow your coronary heart fee, helping to make you experience at peace. During this time of healing rest, you may permit go of worrisome thoughts. It may make revel in for the motive that incense will permit you to lighten up and bring peace to assist with depression and anxiety.

To Practice Mindfulness

When the aroma of severa fragrances enters the air and smells them, they pass thru our noses to our brains. Once the fragrance enters the brain, it motives mind chemical materials that reason pride and one of a kind pleasant feelings. Because you enjoy happier, this permits you to loosen up and become greater aware about your environment.

To Boost Your Sex Drive

Certain scents are considered to be aphrodisiacs because of their aroma. When the fragrance's scent reaches the mind, it reasons the thoughts to supply testosterone that flows to the sexual organs, causing arousal.

Grounding

When you experience a piece out of types or experience like your heads within the clouds, it could be a signal which you need to ground. Certain scents of incense, which include cedar, will assist you revel in extra grounded and once more to yourself.

It Helps You Fall Asleep

Burning incense fills you with a experience of calm. For humans with a difficult time, calmness will help cause drowsiness and assist them fall to sleep. Jasmine is one fragrance that is enjoyable and could assist your thoughts sluggish down and create a experience of peace, permitting you to loosen up and nod off.

Acts As A Natural Air Freshener

Incense can assist to make any room feel fresher. Not in reality in defensive smells however the feeling you get while you walk into it. Because it's all-herbal, no dangerous chemicals are floating spherical inside the debris sprayed into the air.

Candles

We use candles for adornment and aromatherapy; in the past, we used them for an lousy lot greater. Candles have been used considering the start of time. They had been used for plenty ceremonies, from weddings to funerals. Before energy and gas lanterns, candles lit homes. In many cultures, they have been burned in remembrance of these who've handed. Religions have used them for plenty of reasons. Many of the motives are still applicable nowadays. In Christianity, Christ grow to be referred to as the light of the area; candles constitute this. In Judaism, candles are lit as a reminder of the sabbath. In Buddhism, they will be used for nearly all of their ceremonies.

Creates A Place To Relax

Candles use heady scent and mild to create a feel of relaxation inside the room. When the lighting are off, and you have not anything however a smooth flickering glow and a glowing perfume floating via the air, you could't assist but experience comfortable and at peace. Often candles are used by rubdown therapists to assist create a chilled environment in their rooms. Watching the flame of a candle allows to make you revel in comfortable and at peace.

Meditation And Prayer

Candles are believed to create a connection amongst our global and a non secular one. When you moderate one, you are speaking to your self which you are prepared to allow cross of your day and enter right into a peaceful body of mine. Many visualization carrying activities and manifestation techniques include focusing on a burning candle's flame on the equal time as sending your intentions into the universe. Candles are used within the direction of prayer.

Improves Mood

There are many definitely one of a kind scents of candles. The distinct scents can set specific moods. Lavender let you to loosen up after an extended day. Scented candles which include chamomile may additionally have decrease pressure ranges; you want to be extra effective, seize a lemon-scented candle. Cinnamon can assist deliver your mind a lift at the same time as you're beginning to feel the midday drudge.

Romance & Special Occasions

Candles are the conventional way we have an remarkable time birthdays. When you want to have a romantic dinner together with your large wonderful, what's the only problem you do? Light a candle. When you are at a marriage or a wedding dinner, you can probably see candles positioned on tables or lit at a few stage inside the rite.

Stimulates Memory

Similar to incense, extremely good scents of candles can supply lower again memories. An instance of this is that my mother used Jasmine perfume. When I perfume Jasmine, I at once don't forget her. According to The

Harvard Gazette, scent and reminiscence are cautiously related due to how the thoughts is made up.

Self-Expression

We all have things we like greater than others. Picking the ideal candle isn't anyone-of-a-type. There are many scents and designs of candles. Some are available tins, some are available in clean glass containers, while others are available in superbly decorative packing containers. There are candles made for every man or woman type.

How They Help During Meditation

During meditation, you may include crystals, tuning forks, incense, and candles into your bodywork, or use them one after the opposite. No rely the way you pick out to work with them, they may help you've got have been given a meditative restoration experience.

The advantages of the usage of crystals are they assist us become attuned to ourselves. When we preserve precise ones, they invoke precise feelings. Tuning forks create sound vibrations which can launch energy that is stagnant interior of our frame. Incense and candles are similar as they each rely on scents to help set up the room's temper. These items have been used for loads of years in some form or each different in rituals.

Candle staring at is a form of meditation in which you gaze at a lit candle. This sort of meditation lets in to enhance your awareness and your eyesight. If you're interested by starting your 1/three eye or strengthening your instinct, this is an terrific workout to do. This is an reachable meditation to do. You in reality slight a candle, place it at eye level and stare upon the flame. If your interest wanders, definitely supply it lower back.

You can use tuning forks with exclusive system or on their non-public. Some of the benefits of meditating with them are: you switch out to be proper now relaxed, they awaken your proper and left aspect of the thoughts. Tuning forks additionally assist to remove electricity blockages. With the help of a crystal in the form of a Pendulum, you could intention particular regions that are blocked. Once you discover the blockages, you find the right frequency and use the tuning fork to release it.

If you operate incense at some stage in meditation, burn it earlier than meditating so it's going to not problem your breathing. Incense is used to deepen interest and uplift a person's spirit to come to be extra focused and organized to start meditation. Incense creates a temper within the room with the aid of the brilliant scents and the manner they have got an effect on you; as an instance, frankincense is a calming heady scent and a high-quality manner to put together your self.

All of the device brought in this financial catastrophe have comparable benefits plus specific blessings. They all assist in meditation, clean and repel negative energies, supply a experience of peace, and launch pressure.

Chapter 3: What Is A Chakra?

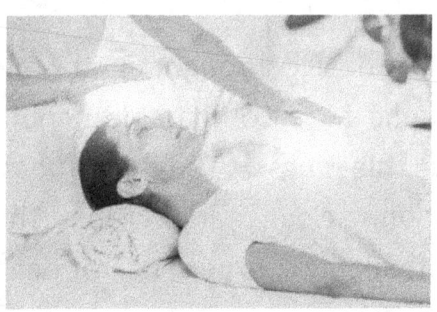

I'm wonderful at one element or some other, you've heard approximately chakras. If you've lengthy beyond to have any form of energy art work finished, the practitioner probable used the word. But do you already know what the phrase manner and definitely how essential it's far? Multiple factors run along our backbone. Most trust we've got got seven chakras, however in fact, there are 12.

When your chakra system is blocked, you will not experience actual mentally or physically. Once you have your first power recuperation consultation, you'll sense the distinction between an open chakra in place of a blocked one. Chakras be a part of, this means that if you stability one, it impacts they all.

Chakra method wheel of slight or spinning disk translated from Sanskrit; this refers to the coloration of the chakra system. Each chakra connects to an organ machine together with our emotional, spiritual, and psychological selves. If virtually this shape of isn't always going for walks right, our whole tool is thrown off.

Chakras are like big storage boxes; they keep our power, mind, emotions, moves, and reviews, every suitable and bad. These existence research help shape our destiny selves. Past memories impact how we examine ourselves and others. From adolescence to adulthood, all of these feelings can cause our chakras to hinder and end up blocked. When chakras are blocked, we've had been given hassle making outstanding selections and may have relational and bodily troubles. There is a combination of things other than the saved feeling which can motive a chakra to emerge as blocked. When we do no longer meet our wishes, we're depressed and don't consume as healthy as we need to.

When the chakras are open and flowing as they have to, you revel in grounded and capable of set healthy barriers. When they may be risky, you experience tired and out of stability. When operating correctly, we have a propensity to miss approximately maintaining our chakras aligned. It is important to maintain our chakras lively and useful; that is how we keep our intellectual interest and stay in concord with ourselves.

The amazing way for us to preserve our chakras balanced and preserve the glide of power moving is to artwork on all factors of our health. Nei Kung is a extraordinary manner to preserve chakras clean and effects maintain the strength flowing. Reiki is each different way to bolster the body's power mission and stability the mind and body.

For a few years there has been now not heaps scientific proof to again up the claims of non secular electricity centers. In the ultimate 5 to eight years, this has changed. Many scientific clinical doctors endorse human beings have some kind of energy recovery in advance than or after surgical remedy.

The Red Chakra is located at the lowest of your backbone. The important reputation of this chakra is the Physical. It's approximately the survival of self and having character dreams met. This chakra is answerable for grounding and a experience of safety. When it's miles open, we revel in safe and degree-headed in our our our bodies. When off-balanced or blocked, you may be indignant or anxious. When the crimson chakra is out of stability, it may cause you to take unique human beings's electricity. The pink chakra connects to all the exclusive chakras; others can not be healthy if that one isn't wholesome.

The Orange Chakra is placed underneath wherein our sexual organs are. The primary attention of this chakra is on Creativity because of the reality sexual electricity is the electricity of advent. It's moreover approximately "we" and the way we interact with others. The orange chakra specializes in Family, Sexual Pleasure and Overall Relationships. When it is open and flowing well it permits you to connect to others and have healthful relationships. When it's far closed, you could have problems along with your feelings. Stifling your creativity will purpose this chakra to end up blocked.

This chakra can emerge as blocked at the same time as there is a lot of discord or trauma inside the circle of relatives or beyond mainly round rape or sexual attack. It is touchy to stress, ailments, and war and these things have a terrible impact on the chakra.

The Yellow Chakra is positioned right above your navel. The awareness of this chakra is "Us" and our conduct in social settings. This chakra is ready being assertive and having a healthy feel of conceitedness. If it's miles overactive, you'll be brash and boastful. If the chakra is underactive, you will be passive. It can emerge as blocked if you have no longer handled your past issues, especially from early life. Can result in conceitedness problems.

The Dantian is the Yellow/Green Chakra and positioned 2 inches under the belly button inward. This chakra is accountable for housing power and it's wherein the twine for Astral Projection is. It is considered to be a middle of qi or existence stress strength and the connection to Nature. When this chakra is blocked or underactive, you could no longer feel grounded or have a Natural sense of protection.

The Green Chakra is located in the chest location. This chakra is about the coronary heart and is the relationship a few of the chakras above and underneath it. This chakra is chargeable for the unconditional everyday love you can offer and get maintain of. When this chakra is wholesome, you're compassionate and loving. When this chakra is overactive, you normally commonly tend to smother people with love. If it's miles below-active, you appear bloodless and aloof. Ways that it may turn out to be blocked is even as you are underneath stress or have a physical contamination.

The Blue Chakra is positioned in the throat. When healthy, you can have a healthy manner of speaking and are constantly honest. If it is underactive, you have a tendency to be extra introverted. If it is overactive, you will speak an excessive amount of and no longer permit others to talk. Not speaking in reality and protecting for your innovative expression will cause problems with this chakra.

The Well of Dreams Chakra is indigo and placed at the lowest of the skull toward the lower back of the neck. When healthy, this chakra will help you advantage a better nation of clairvoyance inside the Dream State and overtly communicate with remarkable dimensions. When underactive or blocked, you can sense worn-out and absence ambition. When overactive, you could have problem telling the distinction amongst reality and creativeness. Lucid dreaming is a advantage of this chakra open.

The Purple Chakra is the 3rd eye and is located among your eyes. This is in which your belief and knowing come from. It's your connection to Magnetism and Electricity. If it's far underactive, you've got got trouble making wholesome alternatives. Also, you will be inflexible in wondering and need to be knowledgeable what to do rather than making healthy picks. When it is overactive, you may live in your fable worldwide and no longer be aware what's round you—a lack of self-self notion, self-doubt, and disability to consider yourself.

The Gold Chakra is positioned at the pinnacle of your head. This chakra is ready Time and the connection to the higher planes thru information and mind, which might be electric powered powered. If it's far underactive, you are not spiritually intuned and have a difficult time connecting with yourself. If it's far overactive, you overthink and intellectualize. Shallow relationships will cause blockages in your crown chakra. Blockages furthermore seem while you worry exchange and repress feelings.

The Silver Chakra is placed round toes. The primary task of this chakra is to preserve your strength flowing with Space and Gravity. When this chakra is wholesome, your charisma is natural, clean, and vivid in coloration.

The Divine Masculine is the Chakra associated with the shade white and located at the proper/dominant hand and is liable for balancing the brilliant strength inside the course of our body. It is controlled via the left hemisphere of the thoughts and specializes within the preference for internal harmony.

The Divine Feminine is associated with the colour black and placed at the left/recessive hand. Similar to the Yang chakra, this chakra is ready influencing traits which is probably considered to be female.

Both the male and female chakras are Yin and Yang and associated with the capability to heal others.

Merkaba is the closes issue to the deliver and correlates with all the chakras and is all through the frame. This is activated at the same time as all of the chakras are wholesome and in balance.

How are they related to the Glands?

The endocrine tool is a few element we normally do not speak about or maybe consider. Perhaps your medical medical physician talks about it all through your each yr checkup. It's genuinely some problem you wouldn't want to take a look at or take a look at about, but it substantially influences our frame and our chakra tool.

There are 8 precise important endocrine structures.

- Hypothalamus
- Pituitary
- Pineal
- Thyroid
- Adrenal
- Pancreas

- Thymus

- Ovaries/Gonads

Each of those has outstanding frame systems they manipulate. The one thing they have got in commonplace is that they secrete hormones to hold our body balanced. These glands release hormones into the bloodstream that assist us with day by day sports activities.

There is a proper away link among the endocrine tool and our chakras. They artwork like companions preserving every special wholesome. If one gland isn't secreting the right amount of hormones, it throws every systems off, and this works the same with the chakras. It is a well-known fact that bodily, highbrow, and emotional health affects our fitness. If they will be now not wholesome, then we can't be healthful.

Both the pituitary gland and the pineal gland adjust the relaxation of the chakra machine's glands. The Hypothalamus and pituitary gland's primary characteristic is to govern the frame's chemistry. They additionally shape a partnership with the pineal gland. The pineal gland's primary undertaking is to make sure all the endocrine structures are in stability with each exceptional. The Thyroid and parathyroid help with metabolism and alter calcium. The Thymus maintains the immune gadget balanced to fight infections. The Adrenal glands play a crucial feature because they help alter hormones that assist manipulate blood strain at a median diploma and help with metabolism. The Pancreas produces insulin that's what's in rate of breaking down sugar. The Ovary and Testis work together to hold gold wellknown sexual and reproductive health.

This now not frequently mentioned tool high pleasant does a number of artwork. We can perform a little simple things to preserve the endocrine and chakra systems strolling their high-quality. Yoga is an superb thrilling manner to stability the chakra structures to keep them flowing. Eating healthful and restricting our intake of sugary food can help keep the endocrine device healthy. Also, our breath may have an effect on how the structures characteristic together.

The pink chakra- connects to the adrenal glands. These glands produce hormones to regulate metabolism, blood pressure, and the immune tool.

The orange chakra - connects to the reproductive glands. And influences each sexuality and hormone secretion.

The yellow plexus - connects to the Pancreas, which permits to modify metabolism through breaking down sugars and fat.

The green chakra - connects to the thymus gland, regulating the immune gadget.

The blue chakra - connects to the Thyroid gland; regulates frame temperature and metabolism.

The puple chakra connects to the Pineal gland, whose number one feature is to provide melatonin, adjust hormones, and assist with coronary heart fitness.

The gold chakra - connects with the Pituitary gland, the grasp gland, regulating all of the glands above.

The crown chakra - connects with the Pituitary gland, the grasp gland, regulating all the glands above.

Chapter 4: What Is Energy?

We recognize as youngsters our parents informed us it changed into a few trouble we had too much of. When we began out faculty, we discovered about the meals pyramid and the way we're capable of have more electricity and be healthy while we comply with it. As we elderly and determined about era, we discovered out that electricity is what we use while we artwork. Later, we located out how an entire lot energy we use is decided through the usage of how a whole lot stress is wanted to do the paintings. The form of power we're going to talk about is some thing special. It is absolutely sitting nonetheless and feeling what's round us and how we enjoy inner of ourselves. Energy is thought thru method of diverse names relying on the subculture; a number of those names are Prana, Mana, Ki, Chi, Cos-mic Force, Lifeforce, Universal Energy.

Our excellent supply of strength is in our minds. It is a wonderful energy deliver that is never-completing. Our thoughts has an inclination to lean toward terrible idea styles out of addiction, but we are capable of trade that sample thru mindfulness. It is hard to trade lifelong practices, in particular when it comes to the mind. You ought to be aware of your thoughts, and at the equal time as you comprehend they will be turning horrible, redirect them.

Energy is likewise referred to as a Universal life strain; it's miles believed this form of energy runs through all residing matters. Most of the power we are capable of communicate about is the type that is not visible however felt. This energy is normally called metaphysical strength.

Have you ever concept of a person sincerely to have them name you or run into them? This is some other shape of energy referred to as intuitive messages and is taken into consideration a type of metaphysical energy. Learning to sense and revel in the electricity is surprisingly smooth to do. It comes glaringly to us, and our body is set up from beginning to do it.

From generation to psychology, there was quite a few research achieved on electricity. While technology can not show metaphysical power exists, it can measure how we reply to power. Both Sir Isaac Newton and Albert Einstein commented on power with the aid of saying it can not be destroyed but modifications and converts from one man or woman to some other.

Best-Selling creator of "Evolve Your Brain: The Science Of Changing Your Mind" Joe

Dizpenza says the Law of enchantment only works even as you positioned out a concept (Electrical) it is strengthened and pulled decrease lower back via your feelings (Magnetic Field)

We are in a steady kingdom of giving and taking electricity. There is an lively law that's called the regulation of enchantment. It says you attraction to what you positioned out. If you are complete of concerned, unhappy power, you may accumulate subjects that make you keep that way. If you could shift your mind to be incredible and glad, you'll collect more happiness. This may additionally additionally genuinely be within the way you be conscious things in preference to receiving. It works in another manner for all and sundry.

Think of a time even as you have were given been in an superb temper. Things were going nicely; your mind became open, you're going with the float, then a person comes round, and it seems like a vacuum just sucked it all out of you. People and conditions motive our strength to empty. This works each methods; there are times we take electricity from others to refill ours. When we experience damage or want to distance ourselves from others, we draw our electricity into ourselves to hold it. When you enjoy your strength start to drain you could repair it with the resource of way of having out in nature. The combination of clean air, sunshine, moonlight, starlight, large our bodies of water, or perhaps leaning in opposition to a tree can upload large portions of power, cleanse, and middle you. Once you've got were given had been given regained your middle and revel in better, you could then do power protective. Energy is neither proper nor lousy, however as an alternative, it's far neutral. We are people who flip the strength first-rate or bad, healthy or bad.

When you recognize strength, you could tell if it is low or sluggish. When your energy is balanced, you make better choices and cope with stress in a healthy manner. People with balanced electricity have an much less difficult time forgiving others due to the fact they are content material in life and understand others may not be. When your religious strength is unbalanced or stagnant, you aren't as able to managing existence's stressors and may turn to pills or alcohol as a way to deal with subjects.

How do you recognize if your energy is balanced or unbalanced? Some humans can tell by means of using seeing colours, and some sincerely apprehend. When you're speakme, in which are your terms coming from? Are they coming from a place of love or a place of anger? What is your aim together in conjunction with your feedback to build up or tear down? When we make alternatives that intend to damage or be awful, that is a clue that our electricity isn't always balanced and may be blocked.

Situations also can have an effect on energy. Think of a time you have got been happy, and everything end up going your manner. How did you experience? Were you smiling? Did you enjoy slight in your feet, your breath flowing unfastened, and your eyes amazing? By searching at you, other humans need to tell with the useful resource of your facial expressions, body stance, and electricity that you were satisfied. Even with out the outward clues, you can tell if the person has top notch electricity. Have you ever walked into a room, and each person have become drawn to as a minimum one individual? That is a reflected image of that individual's power. The contrary is actual furthermore. You can stroll into the room and revel in whom to keep away from at the equal time because the character feels heavy and oppressive whilst you are spherical them. It may also moreover

moreover even be an acquaintance or member of the family that has that form of electricity.

How do electricity blocks take vicinity? There are a few strategies. There are intellectual blocks which might be in which your thoughts is blocked. That comes from black and white, all-or-not something wondering. We make excuses in preference to doing the real paintings. Without give up or take delivery of as genuine with, our power can emerge as blocked. We have an amazing manner to allow move and allow the wonderful come. This is tough to do at times, in particular if we don't feel worth of the best. The way we consider ourselves comes from many exquisite regions of our lives.

When you experience that your energy is becoming worn-out or have an unsightly power change, there are topics you could do. You can also need to make an strength protect. This is even as you area safety of energy round your frame that doesn't allow others' power to come back into contact with yours. That way, you may keep your strength in place of allowing others to take yours.

Here is a easy workout to protect your power. Get into a cushty position wherein you may lighten up. Imagine a vivid moderate going into the top of your head and filling up all spherical you out of your toes and outward. You need it as huge as your arm lengths spread out. It feels heat and comfy, and also you sense consistent. You can take a look at this out with the resource of manner of doing it once in a while. You can exchange the colours and the width. Find what works outstanding for you.

Often people have electricity blocks considering that early life because of the manner their caregiver raised them. Instead of allowing the power to drift, we close it off, so we manage existence. If a infant is punished frequently, they may emerge as afraid of contact. They will begin wondering they will be terrible or do now not understand or understand the motives for the common punishments. These beliefs reason their strength to end up stuck for you to cope with their present day scenario.

That feeling and the manner they deal with existence by no means is going away. You see an lousy lot of the identical behaviors in them now as that they had when they had been youngsters. They stay of their thoughts reading topics in desire to experiencing existence to avoid rejection and humiliation. Their strength stays stagnant and blocked from their early youngsters reviews. They have determined out now not to take opportunities and constantly be on top of things.

As an character, in the event that they realise their strength is blocked and need to exchange it, what can they do? First, they must be organized to get sincere with themselves and be willing to stand their ache. They want to be inclined to permit down the walls and have a look at the locations wherein they don't face fact and distort reality. I as quickly as heard a saying that we don't see subjects as they may be but see them through a clear out of our evaluations. When they open themselves up to start feeling their energy, they may begin to see comparable picks they have got made all through existence, each the good and the awful, and the manner the power has covered them. Once they understand that their patterns are not wanted, they may start converting them. They can thank their herbal defenses for the protection and release them. This isn't an easy technique; it is able to be a long tough one. It commonly takes commonly to try this exercise over and over for it to artwork. From formative years, these patterns have finished out, so there may be a whole existence of restoration desired.

The first step in gaining knowledge of your strength is to pay attention to your mind. Are your mind black and white, or are they open to trade? Do you see subjects as all appropriate or all bad?

During the day, prevent and interest for your body. How are you feeling? Where is your mind? How is your breath? Are you worrying or comfortable? Are you letting a person else take your electricity?

When you float your body, does it sense precise? Does it help you to take away the tension?

When you're with exclusive people, do you experience properly, do you enjoy stressful, pay near interest to how your body feels?

A beneficial factor to do is to discover your power boundaries. When do you enjoy whilst someone comes near you? Do you sense the trade in your energy while someone gets too close to?

A character's physical frame is straightforward to see; you can rapid appearance in the reflect. Instead of specializing in our wishes, we get caught nice looking after our bodily desires. We neglect that we also have energetic goals. While our bodily desires are important, so are our active dreams. This is a 3-detail tool that works together to preserve your energy balanced and going for walks correctly

Energy restoration is a terrific manner to launch saved trauma. This form of recovery works at the aspect of your electricity vicinity to assist restore your frame to a healthful country. Energy recuperation feels brilliant, can be very fun, and receives rid of power blockages. There are a couple of varieties of electricity paintings, studies, ask questions, and find out which one you're maximum interested in.

Working with the chakra gadget is an extremely good way to heal. The chakra device includes 7 critical chakras and 5 chakras you seldom concentrate about. When getting better the chakra tool, the energy worker will normally smooth out your aura first, casting off stored awful strength. Then they may artwork with the chakras. They will begin with the crown chakra first due to the fact that that is the only that controls the relaxation. If that is your first visit, it may take more than one to stability and unblock the chakras. Another issue, the healing is relying on you too. If you get keep of the healing and then pass returned to the identical dangerous behavior and mind, it will not last.

There are numerous strategies to do electricity recuperation. You can do it on your non-public, you can advantage out to an energy healer, or you can have someone use other device which include tuning forks, acupuncture, acupressure, reflexology, and massage.

If you make a decision to go to a practitioner who is an electricity healer, make sure you studies them and ask hundreds of questions. Reiki is a widely known form of power restoration. This recovery kind is even as the practitioner publications power through your body to alleviate blocks and convey balance. The healing typically takes vicinity in a room setup with candles, low lighting, and enjoyable track. The individual receiving the recuperation will lie at the desk, actually dressed and under a sheet or blanket. Once you are mendacity down, the practitioner can have you take a few breaths to loosen up and start the power paintings. Depending at the practitioner, their fingers will contact you lightly or preserve their hands barely above the frame. The healer works from the top of the pinnacle to the ft. Some people experience a warmth emanating from the healer's hands and a relaxing feeling inside the course of their frame; different humans revel in little. Once your restoration is through, the practitioner will provide an motive of what modified into finished and any restoration effects. Usually, the component consequences are much like even as you get a rubdown.

Acupuncture works via setting tiny needles to get power or qi flowing. It dreams precise points on the body and uses the needles to rouse the electricity facilities causing blockages to flow. During the treatment, to stimulate the stressful middle, the practitioner can also moreover twirl or twist the needles. When energy isn't flowing, it reasons human beings to enjoy awful, resulting in illnesses. Acupuncture is stated to assist with many unique conditions and symptoms. Some of them are hypersensitive reactions, headaches, anxiety, melancholy, IBS, and sinus strain.

Full frame acupuncture isn't always the only kind you may reap; there may be now a few different kind referred to as ear acupuncture. Ear acupuncture is primarily based totally really on the principle that your ear's region is attached to a specific organ. This shape of acupuncture is completed by means of putting tiny needles into particular areas in your ear. The practitioner may go away smaller needles referred to as seeds in your ear. These artwork themselves out after a sure amount of time. I even have had this form of acupuncture finished and decided it to be very exciting.

Acupressure is an historic form of Traditional Chinese Medicine that has been used for loads of years. It is just like rub down apart from the purpose of acupressure is to inspire qi (life power) to start moving within the path of the frame and release terrible electricity that has constructed up. Our our bodies have meridians in our our our bodies, and practitioners press on each of those regions to clean any blockages that may have shaped so strength can go together with the drift freely. Acupressure is much like acupuncture in that the practitioners use their arms, arms, palms, and elbows instead of needles to use strain. Acupressure, like reflexology, you may have a touch pain while the stress factors are being worked on, but it have to now not harm; if it does, please allow your practitioner comprehend. There are many first-rate blessings to the use of acupressure, in conjunction with nausea and vomiting, particularly after surgical procedure. It allows with the signs and symptoms and signs and symptoms because of melancholy and anxiety; it lets in relieve headaches and all over again ache.

Reflexology is generally done to the ft. Much like acupressure, it's far believed that particular areas in your feet connect to particular organs and locations on your body. Applying stress to every of these areas is supposed to put off energy blockages to promote healing. Reflexology differs from rub down in the revel in that rubdown is meant to loosen up and decorate move. The purpose of reflexology is to place pressure on precise areas of the foot to enhance the go with the float of qi.

During the remedy, there may be no ache, regardless of the reality that relying on the areas that want healing, there may be slight discomfort because the power is broken up. It want to by no means be painful, so make certain to permit your practitioner understand if you revel in any ache. You have to go away the remedy feeling greater snug; ensure to drink masses of water after receiving remedy.

There are many benefits to reflexology; a number of them beautify your digestive device, alleviate headaches, assist with sinus problems, arthritis, and joint ache. I have been to a reflexologist often and can attest that it has many blessings.

Massage remedy is an umbrella term that carries muscle manipulation of your pores and skin, muscle groups, and tendons to release tension, ache, and pollutants. Many sorts of rub down remedy have tremendous focuses.

Swedish rubdown - This is a rub down that consists of superb rub down techniques which includes kneading, vibration, and tapping. It is a relaxing and mild form of rub down that will help you revel in energized.

Deep tissue rubdown places more stress on muscles to launch muscle tension and promote the recovery of muscle injuries.

Lymphatic drainage – is a slight massage that facilitates to take away the buildup of fluids inside the body. The construct-up of this fluid can exacerbate signs and symptoms and symptoms and signs of a few troubles.

Like many one of a kind recuperation gadget listed above, rub down remedy's benefits are decreasing stress, developing relaxation, relieving ache and pain, and enhancing movement. It may also assist decorate glide, lower coronary heart price, and blood strain. I did not aspect out a few particular massage sorts above, which consist of myotherapy that focuses especially on muscle ache because of the muscle corporations' disorder.

Tuning Forks help to cast off electricity blocks thru the use of vibration and sound to keep power flowing. This shape of recuperation works with every sound and vibration. When the use of the tuning forks for sound remedy, they use distinct frequencies that correspond with the blocked region. Solfeggio Frequencies are tones which have been used for masses of years and are based mostly on 9 tones. Each tone corresponds with chakras that are located in and spherical our our bodies.

Sonotherapy is a form of restoration that combines sound and vibration to promote recuperation on a bodily and subconscious degree. To recognize how sonotherapy works, you want to realize a piece about the Resonance idea. The Resonance Theory is the notion that every organ and frame tool has a herbal vibration and frequency. Healing sounds help get rid of the accumulation of pollution built up over the years because of ailments, trauma, and noise pollutants exposure.

Sound remedy has been used for hundreds of years. If you appearance returned in statistics, you can discover people used it to soothe God and display him reward finally of biblical instances. Native American's used it in masses of 1-of-a-kind ceremonies.

When we are not acting at our first rate, there is a extraordinary danger that our our bodies are not vibrating as they should. Sonotherapy can resolve this and restore harmony. There are many sound remedy types which encompass tuning forks, songs, Tibetan bowls, drums, and so on. Using sound for restoration isn't always intended to invoke emotion, but instead, it is meant to stability and restore.

Weighted Tuning forks are normally placed without delay at the body. These have weights at the forked surrender, and the stem is located to your frame. The weighted tuning forks are beneficial even as you want a more potent vibration. These are regularly used with joint pain and to launch muscle tension.

The chakra tool is an power that runs from your spine to the top of your head. A lot of crucial topics occur on your chakra system. It connects the mind, body, and spirit. If this type of electricity centers isn't functioning successfully, then the whole thing is thrown off. The chakra tool moreover stocks information now not simply from the physical factors of you but moreover the nonphysical.

The charisma is the electricity area that surrounds you and extends out out of your frame. It's thrilling to look at that the whole thing alive has an aura. The air of secrecy changes continuously based for your moods, feelings, and health. There are a couple of layers of the air of mystery. The first is the nearest to your frame and coincides alongside side your physical fitness. The 2nd, called the astral air of mystery, is farther out and displays your emotional country. The following layers are the pinnacle and decrease intellectual auras, one closer to the frame and the other the farthest away. Both of these reflect the idea sorts of your mind and thoughts. The subsequent is the non secular air of secrecy suggests your non secular cognizance, along with information about your intuition. The final layer, the most effective farthest far from the body, balances and integrates all considered one of a kind auroras.

The Meridian device ties your non secular and physical systems collectively. Much much like the chakra device, if one receives blocked, all of them save you strolling efficaciously. You can preserve the ones smooth with the aid of using strategies to get your strength flowing, like acupuncture or acupressure.

Mindfulness is some thing that we can deliver up frequently. It is an crucial part of your daily life. When you are conscious, you take into account to be aware about your frame and what's round you. Mindfulness takes exercising, but it is properly well worth it. If you could set aside a piece every day to recognition and phrase the entirety round you, you may see the advantages are first-rate.

When we aren't well versed in mindfulness, we be conscious something this is going proper away in a 2d or . With mindfulness, you be aware about it without judgment and then allow it pass. You can advantage this whilst you decide which you want to be extra aware of your surroundings. It doesn't have to be crucial which you focus on the small matters which is probably just as critical. Watching a butterfly going from flower to flower is a manner to create mindfulness. Paying hobby to the breath is another manner to acquire recognition. How does your breath enjoy entering into through your nostril, travelling down your frame? Where does it save you? Some people breathe into their stomachs on the equal time as others breathe into their chests.

Grounding is each exceptional mindfulness technique that brings us another time into the winning 2d. Grounding goes in touch with the earth and noticing your environment. When we aren't grounded, we experience almost like we're out of our body. It's tough to attention, and we aren't being attentive to what we are doing. There are many distinctive techniques to ground, and a few might also moreover end up your new preferred hobbies.

A huge key to grounding is feeling yourself related to the earth in some manner. Gardening is a extraordinary manner to ground yourself. You are surely gift in the second, paying attention to what you are doing—strolling or fame outside barefoot is a brief, easy way to floor.

Chapter 5: The Benefits Of An Alkaline Diet

What Is the Alkaline Diet?

The alkaline diet is also known as the acid-alkaline weight loss plan or the alkaline ash weight loss plan. The food plan is primarily based mostly on the concept that the food you eat influences your Ph balance. Once the food is digested, it is believed that it becomes a substance called ash. The ash can be each acidic or alkaline this is absorbed into the bloodstream. Foods which can be much less complicated to digest are considered to be alkaline and motive the frame's Ph decrease. Normal Ph is a choice amongst 7.35-7.Forty five.

Bodies which may be excessive in acid are extra susceptible to ailment and cause emotional issues. Following the alkaline eating regimen will help to raise the Ph balance into the normal variety. The advantages to this are you will be more healthy, you may experience more healthful, and look greater wholesome.

This eating plan has come to be extra well-known due to the fact that celebrities have started out endorsing it. While dropping weight is one advantage of the alkaline diet plan, there are distinct blessings to wholesome-searching pores and skin and usual feeling. As a stylish rule, as soon as celebrities speak approximately products, it makes the recognition increase.

If you're thinking about beginning this eating regimen, there are some things you want to comprehend. While Fresh give up cease end result and veggies make up most of the healthy dietweight-reduction plan, there are various things you need to understand too. First, find out what alkaline and acidic meals are. This may additionally sound smooth, but it isn't. Some meals you will expect had been acidic aren't. Some lists will assist you through the preliminary phase.

Once you discover the alkaline components in preference to which ones are acidic, it's time to shop for what you need. Do now not make the trade . If you do, it is going to be extra hard. If you are making small eating regimen adjustments, it will probable be plenty less complex due to the fact that could be a way of life change and no longer a quick-repair food regimen. Like most way of existence modifications geared within the course of diets, it's far extremely good to make a weekly ingesting plan. Plan your meals, store weekly for the substances you want, and do your remarkable to stay with it. You will slip, and you may have backslides. I advocate, without a doubt, it's tough to disclaim your self precise meals. My weakness is desserts, I can avoid almost some different meals however sit down a brownie within the the the front of me, and I'll consume it.

The top information approximately this lifestyle change is there are not any limits on whilst you can devour, like intermittent fasting. But there are some things you want to understand. You can consume additives that are alkaline, impartial and restriction those which can be acidic. Typically the ratio is 70:30, with 70% of your weight-reduction plan which encompass alkaline and 30% of acidic meals.

Below are some mind on what you want to and shouldn't eat:

prevent cease end result

vegetables

soybeans

seeds

legumes

tofu

Most importantly, drink more water; You can upload lemon or lime to it.

This won't sound like an awful lot range, but after you have got a study the recipes, you can see there can be.

Food that you have to save you (undergo in mind 70:30 ratio)

dairy merchandise, together with cheese and butter

processed meals

eggs

pork

fowl

grains

fish

espresso

alcohol

soda

The elements at the lists of ones you may devour and ones you want to restriction are in particular confusing. There are some acidic culmination and veggies but, after digestion, do not go away acid inside the frame. That is the number one cause that having a list of meals can be beneficial, especially in the beginning.

Fruits and Vegetables are crucial to have for a balanced healthy dietweight-reduction plan. While many fruits are discouraged in the Alkaline healthy dietweight-reduction plan, there are also many fruits you're advocated to eat. Fruits which include lemons, limes, and oranges are a number of the nice ones to eat. They detox the body in fact and help relieve and save you heartburn. You can devour maximum melons, berries, pears, pineapple, cherries, and so forth.

Vegetables are important on your fitness. They are packed complete of vitamins and feature just a few calories. This is why many diets advocate you fill your plate with veggies whilst having smaller portions of other meals. You are encouraged to eat an extended listing of greens - vegetables, broccoli, cabbage, celery, inexperienced beans, and mushrooms. There are many more which is probably at the list as well.

Soy, soda, espresso, junk food, and candy are meals to keep away from on the alkaline weight loss plan. Soy carries compounds that impact hormone degrees and are significantly processed. Highly processed substances are some difficulty that desires to be avoided. Soda, sweet, and junk meals have a high sugar content cloth and characteristic many chemical compounds in them which is probably horrific. Coffee and soda are every pretty acidic and need to be avoided.

Benefits to Eating an Alkaline Diet

Weight Loss - Changing your food plan from excessive sugar over-processed factors will reduce the full-size type of electricity you're eating. Weight loss is due to burning extra strength than you devour. Developing this eating addiction will help you devour fewer electricity, ensuing in weight loss.

Preventing Cancer - Eating a healthy dietweight-reduction plan decrease in meat and extra give up result and vegetables can also moreover decrease the chance of maximum cancers. Also, reducing the quantity of caffeine and soda can also decrease the opportunities too.

Treating Or Preventing Heart Disease - because the diet is low in fat and calories, it promotes a greater in shape way of life and might decrease your threat of coronary coronary heart illness.

Improving Growth Hormone Levels - on the same time as there can be no conclusive evidence, studies have tested that limiting acidic additives will assist decorate boom hormone stages.

Improving lower again pain studies shows that alkaline may additionally additionally assist to relieve once more pain. A diet excessive in acidic food lowers the amount of magnesium this is superior. Magnesium is essential to pain control. Eating a food regimen with many fruits and vegetables permits with magnesium manufacturing. Magnesium permits to deliver more food plan D, which is also vital in ache control.

Improves Kidney Health - lowering acidic stages in urine makes an unfriendly surroundings for crystallization to occur. Eating a diet excessive in alkalic food moreover reduces the quantity of hard work your kidneys want to do to clear out the blood. While a weight-reduction plan change will no longer treatment kidney sickness, it may sluggish down the contamination.

Fights Against Fatigue - give up end result and greens surrender strength to make revel in that it might increase our energy stages. Levels of oxygen boom, so oxygen and this has an instantaneous courting to power tiers.

Helps With Healthy Muscle Development- a small good sized shape of studies have confirmed that a low acidic diet helps growth muscle mass. Eating processed substances and growing the quantity of fruit and veggies moreover help for muscle improvement.

Strengths Immune System - this comes decrease lower back to right vitamins and digestive fitness. People frequently overlook approximately how critical a healthful digestive tract is. It no longer simplest facilitates along side your immune device, however it additionally impacts your moods, your power, and the way sturdy your immune machine is. Alkaline food is less complicated to break down, inflicting a extraordinary deal less stress for your digestive machine.

Reduces Inflammation - Too hundreds acid within the frame can reason contamination. Diseases which consist of coronary heart illness and arthritis are because of contamination. When a diet is complete of wholesome food, this decreases your infection. Eating many oils and fat reasons inflammation to stand up; this is how the frame lowers infection.

Oral Health - a weight loss plan rich in acidic meals devour away at teeth enamel. This reasons tooth to become sensitive, will boom your chances of getting cavities and the way prolonged your enamel will final.

You can discover extra information about the Alkaline weight loss plan through using looking up studies that Dr. Sebi executed.

Sun Light, Moonlight, and Nature Good for Your Energy Body

Humans' dating with the sun has been spherical because of the truth the start of time. It has been used to tell the time, maintain tune of the seasons, and is worshiped in some religions. The solar in greek mythology end up respected as one of the gods; Greeks moreover shared legends to educate training. Native Americans informed the solar's memories, God for schooling schooling to the kids; they believed that there could not be life with out the solar. The pagans worshiped the sun, constructed altars to offer gives to the sun god, and had fairs for celebrations. In Kemet, additionally called Egypt/Hikuptah, they believed that the sun might in all likelihood die each night and are available back to life each day. To them, this become a sign of immortality. Nomads and historical Koreans celebrated the solar because it supplied warm temperature and power. In statistics, some accept as real with the sun is God because of references to Heaven and the world as a lamp at his ft. The Bible makes many references to lamps, Christ being the mild of the world, and the sun presents that slight.

Without the sun, there might be no life. The solar presents warmth to the location, that is crucial to photosynthesis, and this is wanted for vegetation to make bigger. The sun regulates the snow, rain, and similar weather. The majority of human beings recognize that rain is created by using way of the sun, inflicting evaporation this is absorbed through using the usage of clouds, and once they get full, they release it within the form of rain, snow, and so forth. The solar impacts the climate and the climate, relying on how close to you are to the sun.

It has been scientifically validated that the sun has many advantages. It is our primary supply of eating regimen D, that could assist save you many ailments and ailments. It's a herbal antidepressant; through growing Vitamin D, you're glaringly boosting your serotonin levels. Lower degrees of serotonin have a proper away courting with despair. You can take vitamins D in the shape of nutritional dietary dietary supplements, but your body doesn't soak up them as well. Increasing the quantity of diet D absorbed benefits sexual fitness due to the powerful consequences on sex hormones. The extended testes/ovary health helps to maintain the sacral chakra flowing freely.

The pineal gland is called the mild of the thoughts. Being uncovered to the solar will maintain this vicinity of the mind healthy and walking because it need to. According to Scientific American, People with regular nutrients D stages have better cognitive feature than those with lower ranges. To get the solar's complete advantages for the pineal gland and mind, you may do a non secular workout called solar looking— sungazing is the workout of sitting within the sun and searching it. The first-rate instances of day to do which can be at sundown and sunrise. It is not solid to do this workout while the solar is full and surprisingly vibrant.

Take off your shoes and stand collectively together with your toes right away on the ground. During the wintry weather, feel loose to face barefoot in your home and gaze at the sun. Without carrying glasses or contacts, gaze at the solar. Blink your eyes at a natural charge. There's no need to stare. When your thoughts wanders, genuinely convey it back to searching the solar and your breath. Think about all of the approaches the sun benefits. You will experience the texture of it to your face. You do no longer have to gaze for any precise length of time; genuinely do it for so long as you feel snug. When you're executed, you could say a prayer, near your eyes gently and pass on approximately your day. Your imaginative and prescient can be off for a few minutes after solar searching at, that is everyday. The exceptional times to sun gaze are the Golden Hours, Sun Rise till hours after, and hours earlier than Sunset.

In addition to the highbrow and emotional benefits of the sun, there also are non secular advantages. Earlier, I wrote approximately how the sun allows stimulate the pineal gland. This gland is wherein our natural abilities are developed. The spiritual capabilities are intuition and clairvoyance. Intuition is the potential to apprehend sure subjects without being knowledgeable.

An example of that is one I used in advance while you are considering someone regularly and then strolling into them. Intuition is likewise called having a intestine feeling. Clairvoyance honestly technique clear seeing. This is while someone definitely seems to realize things without being told. Typically the statistics includes them in a few shape of metaphor. Being able to see someone's charisma is an instance of clairvoyance.

No depend in that you live, you have a hazard to enjoy the sun. When you are in your way home or to your manner to paintings, take a few minutes definitely to face out of doors, improve your face to the sun and only take in a number of its natural recuperation energy. Taking the time to stand inside the sun will assist you to enjoy greater lively and in a better temper.

Another easy meditation you could do is pass sit down down out of doors, ideally at the floor, but if you may't, draw close a chair. Set along side your legs skip-legged or firmly at the ground. Make first-rate you are going thru the solar, then near your eyes. Place your palms to your legs, hands dealing with up alongside aspect your thumb and second finger touching. While sitting there, simply feel the sun on your face. You will find out it interior a couple of minutes; you could find out your mind settled and genuinely enjoy higher. The solar additionally lets you easy your air of secrecy and stability your chakras. The most easy manner to try this is through a series of Tai Chi movements that includes a series of frame movements.

We had all skilled troubles in existence at the same time as we had little desire left. The rainbow in lots of cultures is an indication of recent beginnings that the whole lot is probably k and correct accurate fortune. There are some one-of-a-kind varieties of rainbows. The one I need to inform you about is the whirling rainbow, the aura of the moon. The whirling rainbow appears similar to the rainbow ring during the solar on a cloudy gray day. It is a promise in Native American's prophecy that we're capable of all be identical in the end, and this could be a time of peace, love, and desire. The whirling rainbow is sent to remind of this time and supply need. To keep in thoughts the colors of the rainbow, we are able to use the acronym Roy-G-Biv - which stands for purple, orange, yellow, green, blue, indigo, and violet.

Moonlight is a mirrored photo of the solar's mild inside the darkness. Thus, there may be a combining of the masculine strength from the sun and the moon's female energy. Combining the ones two energies encourages us to achieve this after which lighten up and appearance beforehand to the outcomes. Moonlight offers us a enjoy of awe and allows us revel in a extra connection to the universe.

Moonlight allows us see awesome regions wherein we want to trade and begin the exchange. If feasible, try and bypass outdoor at night time to take within the moon's strength. Moonlight has many spiritual and fitness blessings. Moonlight lets in to lighten up us and permits to decrease depression with the useful useful resource of growing endorphins. These endorphins help to decrease blood pressure and help to modify the menstrual cycle.

The moon's power, if no longer used nicely, can reason chaos and disruption too. Have you ever heard the pronouncing whilst a hard and fast of peculiar subjects take location inside the course of the day that "it want to be a complete moon?"

Moonbathing is much like sunbathing, moon bathing is a way to take inside the electricity of the moon. The great time to do that is the various waxing and entire moon. Moonbathing is really going outside at night time time and basking in the moon's power. You need to spend at the least half of-hour connecting to the moon's energy. It may have a completely calming and fun impact if you want to result in a better night time's sleep. I

Moongazing, like sun looking, is a way to advantage the benefits of the moon's strength while meditating. If you can skip out of doors to gaze at the moon gaze, if not stand or take a seat via a window to experience the moon's mild. You in reality permit the moon's slight and electricity fill you. Gaze up at the moon for so long as you're able.

The first gain from moon looking at is which you get outdoor into nature that is a healing gain. Research has demonstrated that individuals who stargaze have extended emotions of happiness, rest, and peace.

Understanding The Moon Cycle

It takes 28 days for the moon to rotate throughout the solar; because the moon turns, its mirrored image is decided thru its relation to the solar. When you have a observe the moon at night time, you notice the sunlight's reflected photograph at the moon emitting a glow. It's much like the earth's night time time time moderate.

New Moon

In this segment, you aren't capable of see the moon. The darkish sky is thought to suggest a cutting-edge beginning. It is a time to make a glowing begin, inclusive of new friendships, new conduct, and set easy intentions. This is an remarkable time to meditate and create new goals.

New Moon Meditation- make a listing of goals which you need to reap inside the next 30 days. Make certain they may be capacity. You're not probably to turn out to be a millionaire in 30 days except you hit the lotto or a few detail similar.

Waxing Crescent

The waxing crescent is wherein the moon isn't quite entire but is operating its manner there. It is constructing up electricity and moving earlier. Meditating presently lets you maintain shifting forward entire of need. Pass outside within the moonlight for ten mins each night time. The moon bathing will assist to preserve you energized and moving in advance to show up your purpose. With the contemporary-day power that the waxing crescent moon creates, you can start manifesting your desires from your listing.

First Quarter

The first area moon is also referred to as the half of-moon. This is a time of severe interest. You have completely centered on your intentions and are walking at them at entire stress. This is also an first-rate time to re-evaluate in that you are and what you need for the future. Keep transferring earlier - do now not permit doubt and fear save you you currently.

Waxing Gibbous

This moon is often called the ¾ moon. This is a level for further improvement which you need to do for the manifestations you wrote sooner or later of the complete moon. You can also refine and plan what moves are essential to complete your desires. This is also a time to meditate on things you want to benefit, like new friends, a modern activity, or have a observe a contemporary exchange or hobby.

Full Moon

This is the segment wherein the moon and solar are in ideal alignment. From right proper here, the moon will become smaller until the ultra-modern moon segment is reached. This is the time while the moon has the most massive energy. Crystals can be cleared and recharged proper now with the resource of placing them within the moonlight. This is time for guidance, healing, and magic.

The full moon is the exquisite time for clearing bad or stagnant energy. You can do both a bodily cleaning and an power clearing. The strength clearing is achieved through smudging; you can do that in lots of particular techniques, with incense, sage, or a few other way making a decision upon.

Here is a brief release meditation you may do in your new cleansed area:

Write down on paper a listing of things (feelings, emotions, and many others.) you need to take away.

Light a candle - I choose the color based totally at the topics I need to remove; one-of-a-type human beings have preferred shades they choose to paintings with. Light the candle, recognition on the flame, and examine your list. Meditate at the candle, burn the paper and throw the ashes away.

You can do a gratitude ritual in a comparable way aside from you want to put in writing belongings you're thankful for and what you have got completed. Let the paper take a seat down down in the moonlight to percent your gratitude.

Waning Gibbous

This is even as the slight of the moon begins to lower. It isn't always as large. This is an amazing time to meditate on lousy behavior you need to quit, consciousness on releasing strain and poor questioning.

Third Quarter

This is the time whilst you want to relaxation for a piece after which plan your subsequent steps. This is a top notch time for aware meditation. You can start setting some new dreams and new intentions.

Waning Crescent Moon

This is the last section earlier than the extremely-cutting-edge moon. Rethink what you want, what desires you need to set, and acquire. Rest and take masses of time finding out what it is you want

The Body And Spiritual Anatomy

Spiritual anatomy is the idea that the body and spirit are related. This way that mind and studies, high-quality or terrible, directly have an effect on the frame's fitness. Our reviews from youth to the prevailing go away imprints in our our bodies that effect physical and non secular health.

Negative critiques should have an effect at the body in masses of strategies. Stress harms our immune device. An immune system not working correctly leaves us open to many illnesses. In contemporary years there was extra clinical studies in how saved trauma manifests itself no longer best mentally however bodily.

The trauma doesn't ought to be a single catastrophic occasion along side a twister, abuse, storm, or near-demise experience. It moreover can be due to many small activities, together with a breakup, a go with the waft, or undertaking loss. Most trauma will remedy on its very personal in a few months. When trauma doesn't remedy on its very personal, humans get caught in the flight, flight, or freeze reaction.

When the frame perceives a hazard, the involved device goes to paintings; if the man or woman cannot control it, it's going to begin the fight, flight, or freeze reaction. This response raises tension, will increase coronary heart rate, there's a surge of adrenaline. Some people get stuck in this reaction. They are normally demanding and geared up for some thing wrong to take region. This is at the same time as the feelings, feelings, and sports turn out to be stored in the body bodily and mentally. The disturbing power is now stored in our frame and emotional systems. The power storage will become stuck in our our our bodies. When recalled, the memory will produce the same type of response over and over. The consistent recurrence prevents recuperation from the trauma without help.

Our body is lots extra unexpected than we offer it credit score score for. It can heal itself, it may hold memories, and it has an incredible communication gadget. Trauma is going deeper into the frame than most recognize. The cells saved in the reminiscences can pop out as chronic ache like once more ache, muscle pain within the frame. The cells reason belief troubles too. This comes out as irrational fears like you've got been bit by using way of a dog and are in truth afraid of all dogs.

The equal as emotional imprints stay on your mind, bodily imprints form for your cells. When you could deal with the trauma and heal it, then like your thoughts, the cells will heal too. Many treatments can offer you with remedy and can help you heal.

Combining holistic and conventional treatments are the quality strategies to begin the recovery. Conventional remedy is extra for treating illnesses or chronic ailments. It might be a better idea to go a unique route for trauma recovery.

When you talk about the reminiscences and start feeling them in your frame, you could heal from the trauma. There are many forms of therapists, a few aggregate holistic practices on the facet of speakme. Those are my personal opportunities. They use inner infant paintings, strength art work, and help with boundaries. It is crucial to art work through recollections; satisfactory then can you work on recognition and restoration.

The holistic approach consists of many things. Tai Chi and particular styles of workout are remarkable for supporting to locate where mobile memories are saved on your body and launch it. Sometimes, you'll find out a stretch at the way to discover excessive first-rate moves which will cause an emotional reaction whilst doing great sports sports. This is part of the muscle memory walking itself out. It can also purpose subjects to come returned lower back up; you could turn out to be emotional or maybe cry. That's ok; it's far commonplace as part of your adventure.

Meditation and mindfulness will help you find wherein recollections are saved, and you can paintings thru them with breathwork or extraordinary freeing techniques. This may additionally carry up feelings too. This is everyday; it is your thoughts running thru the trauma. The first year I began meditating and spent my first year being very touchy to my environment and the inner me. The recovery benefits were actually really worth it.

Massage and acupuncture are one-of-a-type high-quality alternatives to release memories locked in cells. With rub down, they're running with muscle tissues to launch anxiety and pollution within the body. Acupuncture goals particular areas of the body to unfastened electricity blockages.

If you do the work incorporating extra than one of the trauma remedy alternatives, it will in all likelihood be clearly well worth it. There are 4 ranges to trauma recuperation. Stage one is understanding you're now steady. Feeling secure is likewise connected for your first chakra, the muse. Meditation is a excellent manner to begin to revel in strong. Step is mourning what passed off. This degree may also additionally development slowly. This is about remembering and running to heal and go together with the glide thru it too. Reconnect on the aspect of your new self. You had been capable of take delivery of what befell, mourn, and look at a new manner to cope with it. Now you accept who you've got got grow to be. It isn't always approximately returning to who you have been but rather growing whom you are. The final stage is to keep growing into whom you have grow to be.

Chapter 6: What Are Chakras?

Chakra, which comes from the Sanskrit word for "wheel," describes its feature perfectly. People who consider that the chakras are spinning disks of electricity that, while "open" and aligned, promote pinnacle-nice highbrow, emotional, and physical fitness don't forget themselves in bliss. Uneven physical, mental, or emotional health may additionally come from blocked chakra strength. Worry, exhaustion, and digestive issues are certainly a number of the severa trouble effects you'll be experiencing. A properly-rounded asana exercising can launch energy and stimulate an imbalanced chakra, facilitating the profound inward modifications for which yoga is identified. With a chunk steering, the Chakras can become a exceptional device for channeling your power in your preferred route.

Understanding the Chakras

Your yoga practice can be taken into consideration because the architect responsible for bringing the chakra device into physical manifestation. Learning how each chakra relates to a pleasing detail in the natural international is the maximum honest approach to position them to use. Earth, water, air, fireside, and ether correspond to the primary 5 chakras (or place). Since the ones remaining chakras are alleged to link us to dimensions beyond our very own, moderate and cosmic strength are frequently associated.

The detail related with each chakra will let you enjoy that detail's presence for your frame. You may find out extra energy at your disposal by using reinterpreting your bodily shape within the ones symbolic terms. The earth detail is associated with the lowest chakra. When it is in check, we enjoy powerful and strong; on the identical time as it's out of whack, we should experience ungrounded and dangerous.

Another instance might be the water-related pelvic chakra. When it's miles in check, we enjoy supple, and our imaginations run wild. When it is not, we are able to feel like a plant that hasn't been given enough water: brittle, dry, and probable even inflexible?

You have a series of power centers known as chakras from the lowest of your spine to the pinnacle of your head.

Root Chakra = Muladhara

Sacral or Pelvic Chakra = Svadhisthana

Navel Chakra = Manipura

Heart Chakra = Anahata

Throat Chakra = Vishuddha

Third-Eye Chakra = Ajna

Crown Chakra = Sahasrara

Chakras are taken into consideration to be power centers in each Hinduism and

Buddhism. They denote the meeting of numerous kinds of non secular power. According to a 2019 evaluation of the records of Chakras, this is due to the similarity among chakras and spinning wheels or discs. Energy is despatched from one supply to every one-of-a-kind through channels among wheels.

The early Hindu thoughts of a bodily body and a subtle frame are associated with the idea of Chakras. The physical frame is made from mass and is clearly obvious to the bare eye. However, the diffused frame, which encompasses the mind and the emotions, is crafted from electricity and isn't always. In this version, the subtle body acts as a conduit for spiritual or psychic electricity to have an impact on the gross frame and vice versa. This indicates that a person's health and properly-being is probably affected by the condition of their chakras.

It is frequently held that a sequence of power facilities known as chakras run vertically from the crown of the pinnacle to the tailbone. However, the quantity of chakras someone has can also exchange relying on their precise spiritual exercise. There are 4 most important chakras, steady with Buddhist concept. Typically, in Hinduism, there are seven. According to nice traditions, there are hundreds of electricity facilities, however best a pick out out quantity topics. The seven-Chakra paradigm is the most famous Western framework.

In Hinduism, the ones energy facilities are referred to as Chakras, and there are various more than just the seven critical ones. Here are some of the maximum critical ones:

The Muladhara, or root chakra, is placed the diverse anus and genitalia at the lowest of the backbone. Sex, meals, sleep, and the need to stay to inform the story are only a few of the primal wishes that it's miles said to have an effect on.

The sacral chakra (Svadhisthana) is positioned in the lower abdomen and regulates the body's emotional and sexual desires.

Manipura, regularly known as the navel chakra, is located subcutaneously. Having a wholesome 0.33 chakra opens the door to higher digestion and assimilating lifestyles's training.

The coronary heart chakra is within the center of the chest and serves as a portal to the arena of unconditional love.

The Vishuddha (throat) chakra is placed at the lowest of the cranium and is chargeable for the free expression of one's actual self.

The Third Eye chakra is in the space among your eyebrows and is the supply of your attention and attention.

The Sahasrara crown chakra, placed on the very pinnacle of the pinnacle, is accountable for encouraging a greater spiritually enlightened outlook on life.

The Chakras are strength vortexes at normal intervals alongside the spinal column. The first chakra, the foundation chakra, is located on the identical level because the coccyx and is the element of connection many of the character and the soil. The 2d, or sacral, chakra is located right now underneath the navel. The sun plexus chakra is the 0.33 and lowest within the stomach. The coronary coronary heart chakra is positioned at the bodily internet web page on line given that name; the second one chakra is the throat. Then, barely above the eyebrows, the 0.33 eye chakra beckons you interior and permits you're making contact with unseen forces. The very last chakra is the crown chakra, placed on the very top of the top.

Traditional Indian medication, often called "ayurvedic remedy," is based mostly on those power factors. Chakra is Sanskrit which means "wheel," a language used for over five thousand years in India to transmit spiritual teachings. Many Sanskrit terms, consisting of "Buddha," "Himalaya," and "Yoga," have entered the English lexicon. Nearly 88,000 chakras, which encompass the seven primary ones, make up those energy facilities unseen to the bare eye.

The vibrational strength received and emitted with the useful resource of method of these seven strength wheels impacts our bodily systems and feelings. The vibrational frequency of the chakra is contemplated in its colour. Each chakra has a very precise coloration: pink for the idea chakra, orange for the sacral chakra, yellow for the sun plexus, green for the coronary heart, and turquoise for the throat after the 1/three eye's indigo comes the crown chakra's mauve.

The decrease chakras are associated with our baser dispositions, whereas the pinnacle chakras are related to our better religious selves. The energy that permeates our our our bodies may be visualized as a ray of moderate that travels up the spine from the bottom chakra to the crown chakra on the top of the top. This ascending spiral of moderate connects the physical worldwide to the heavenly realm. Feeling this energy undergo us from the floor up is how we connect to the cosmos. When the passage of this mild stress is unobstructed from one wheel to the following, our chakras are aligned, and we are comfortable.

Negative emotions, like pressure, infection, or even unresolved past injuries, disrupt this energy go with the float, inflicting bodily and intellectual contamination. Yoga, meditation, and chakra alignment with crystals are only some of the options for locating equilibrium once more after experiencing such negative sports. Due to the crystal's harmonious vibration, the Chakras can realign and find out their finest frequency. When functioning commonly, the chakras invite this existence strain in and delivery it from one strength middle to some other, continuously in an upward trajectory from the ground to the skies. Having "balanced chakras" commonly refers to being in exact bodily, highbrow, and emotional shape. Besides, what else is there to say?

The Chakras are strength vortexes at regular durations alongside the spinal column. The first chakra, the inspiration chakra, is positioned on the identical diploma because of the fact the coccyx and is the issue of connection a few of the man or woman and the soil. The 2d, or sacral, chakra is located at once below the navel. The solar plexus chakra is the 1/3 and lowest within the belly. The coronary heart chakra is placed on the bodily net web page for the motive that call; the second one chakra is the throat. Then, barely above the eyebrows, the 1/3 eye chakra beckons you within and enables you are making contact with unseen forces. The very last chakra is the crown chakra, located at the very pinnacle of the pinnacle.

History of Chakras

You probably discovered about Chakras from your yoga trainer or reiki hold near in case you ever participated in a hard and fast meditation or obtained a consultation lasting extra than an hour. My yoga teacher frequently discusses the 0.33-eye chakra, it truely is located a number of the brows, and explains that it is the seat of human instinct and the inner mild. Sure, you pay hobby approximately chakras, but what are they, exactly?

According to the Chopra Center, there are seven chakras, or non secular energy facilities, in a few unspecified time inside the future of the backbone, the neck, and the crown of your head. The word "chakra" comes from the idea Sanskrit word for "wheel" or "disk." The earliest document, the Vedas, which describes the chakra tool, dates decrease once more to historical India, perhaps amongst 1500 and 500 B.C., "in step with Yoga Master and Reiki Healer Fern Olivia. The Vedas are Hinduism's holiest scriptures, written in Sanskrit distinctly early. What, exactly, are the seven chakras for? "They every correspond to excessive fine organs further to physical, emotional, psychological, and non secular states of being and effect all elements of your lifestyles," explains Olivia. Prana, the final herbal recovery pressure, is located in each of those chakras and flows from the universe outward and internal us to keep our fitness, happiness, and electricity normally. The notion that non secular strength can be felt physical is imperative to studying the seven chakras and training reiki, yoga, and great modalities that emphasize chakra alignment. "When our chakras are balanced and open, prana can float freely via them, allowing our power to waft freely. However, you need to have a corporation draw close to of the fundamentals of every chakra in advance than proceeding to a better exploration.

Six matters approximately the Chakras you need to understand but possibly do not.

The concept of the chakras, or diffused power factors in the frame, has captured Western creativeness greater than almost some other education from the Yoga way of life at some diploma inside the beyond hundred years. However, the West (besides for a few college students) has nearly truely did not apprehend what the chakra concept intended in its authentic context and the manner one is expected to artwork with them. I'm going to bypass the advent and jump right into the list of the six maximum essential data approximately the chakras that most present day yogis have overlooked.

The term "chakra" wants to be defined first. Chakras (Skt. Chakra) are electricity formations equal to discs or plants at the internet web sites in which several channels or meridians converge and feature focal elements for meditation in the Tantrik traditions from whence the term originates. They are conceptual structures however additionally phenomenologically based surely. They have a tendency to be placed wherein human beings experience emotional and/or religious power, and the shape in which they may be visualized shows the visionary reviews of meditators.

(As I referred to, Western way of lifestyles has but to absolutely draw near chakras. More exactly, once I discuss with "the West," I suggest European and American traditions and elements of cutting-edge Indian lifestyle that draw thought from Western traditions. I encompass most of the contemporary-day English-language teachings on yoga in India in my definition of "Western" due to the fact it's far now almost impossible to find out a fashion of yoga in India that Euro-American beliefs have now not impacted about it.

Okay, I'll be honest: Western yoga is aware about very little approximately the chakras, no matter the truth that this know-how modified into considered vital via the ancient subculture. You see, in case you examine a few aspect like the Wheels of Life through Anodea Judith, you want to apprehend which you are not analyzing a piece of yoga philosophy but as an alternative a piece of Western occultism based totally on the subsequent 3 assets: The Chakras (1927) through Theosophist C.W. Leadbeater is an example of an early artwork of Western occultism that borrows and adapts Sanskrit terms without definitely facts them. Only the scholarly community has get proper of access to to books approximately the chakras based on an intensive facts of the historic Sanskrit texts.

"Is that even applicable?" yogis regularly are attempting to find advice from me on severa subjects. Don't forget about that I profited masses through analyzing Anodea Judith's e-book and others find it irresistible! That's no longer going to appear, nor will it appear to me. If you claim to have benefited from some factor, it need to be proper irrespective of where it got here from. I handiest have subjects to mention: first, modern Western authors at the chakras who declare to be imparting historical teachings are lying to you. They actually do not apprehend it given that they cannot have a examine the reliability in their supply materials (because of the truth they do not look at Sanskrit). Secondly, as a Sanskrit student and a yogi who prefers classical practices, I'm happy to shed a few slight on the this means that that of yogic phrases of their authentic context for everybody curious. You on my own recognize fine whether or not or now not or not or now not that lets in you. I am no longer arguing that age itself confers any sort of advantage. By no method am I suggesting that Western occultism is without benefit on a non secular degree? I'm doing the first-rate I can to deliver the essence of the beyond in easy English. Now I shall visit the six rudimentary facts regarding the chakras that most modern-day yogis have left out.

1. In the authentic lifestyle, there may be multiple chakra device.

Too many! During its heyday between 600 and 1300 CE, Tantrik Yoga superior a concept of the diffused body and its electricity centers called chakras (or padmas (lotuses), dhras, laksyas (focal elements, and masses of others.). This subculture is still practiced nowadays. After 900 CE, on the equal time as Tantrik Yoga became honestly advanced, many colleges articulated their particular chakra tool, with a few faculties articulating many systems. The form of chakras taught also can range from 5 to 20-one, depending on the scripture and the lineage being studied. The seven(or nicely six-plus-one) chakra machine acquainted to Western yogis is exceptional certainly considered one in all many, and it started out to predominate across the 15th century.

I can nearly listen your subsequent question: "But which system is accurate?" 'Are there severa chakras?' Herein lies the supply of the initial communique breakdown. Chakras are not like physical factors; they are now not tough truths that can be studied inside the same way that, say, neuronal ganglia are (with which the chakras had been difficult within the nineteenth century). Like each non-material, non-realistic fact, the strength body (sukshma-sharira) is fantastically malleable. Depending at the character and the shape of yoga exercising being undertaken, incredible strength facilities can also moreover seem in a single's enjoy of the energy frame.

While one-of-a-type cultures may additionally have unique beliefs approximately in which these facilities are located, most agree that they're positioned within the decrease stomach (the sexual center), the heart, and the crown of the top. These are the 3 locations on the body in which humans everywhere revel in emotions and feature non secular recollections. Aside from the Big Three, the actual texts gift a remarkably severa array of chakra systems. No one way of doing some thing is inherently advanced to a few exceptional. In a five-detail practice, for instance, you may hire a 5-chakra device. One uses a six-chakra tool to channel the strength of six separate deities. Naturally, right? However, Western yoga has but to seize without delay to this essential records. The journey down the rabbit hole has just started, Alice. Care to discover greater? Okay, now, onto the second one.

Two, the chakra systems are normative rather than explanatory. This is a chief attention. Some English-language articles address the chakras as objectively actual, describing their places and sunglasses (e.G., "the muladhara chakra is high-quality at the bottom of the human spine and is pink"). Most of the genuine Sanskrit texts, however, do no longer educate us on the man or woman of fact hundreds as they provide us with a specific yogic exercise: we are to anticipate a subtle item made of colored moderate, fashioned like a lotus, or a spinning wheel, positioned at a factor inside the body, after which spark off mantric syllables in it. This clarifies my in advance thing #1. The writings prescribe movements one need to take to perform a positive give up thru mystical technique. "The yog need to image a 4-petaled lotus..." is what we're expected to make out of the elliptical "four-petaled crimson lotus at the lowest of the body" within the unique Sanskrit. For similarly explanation on this, please go to aspect #five beneath. The mental states related to the chakras are definitely cutting-edge and Western.

The muladhara chakra is related to safety and survival, the manipura chakra with the electricity of man or woman and a healthy experience of self confidence, and so forth, regular with myriad internet web sites and books at the state of affairs. Any self-respecting yogi definitely nicely really worth his or her salt is aware about that linking the chakras to emotional or mental states is a quite current Western invention that may be traced once more to Carl Jung. Such institutions may additionally moreover replicate actualities inside the lives of certain humans (despite the fact that seldom with out priming), however we do not find them in the Sanskrit texts. However, one exquisite exception is the 10-chakra device for yogi-musicians, which I've written about on my blog. However, within the device evolved in the thirteenth century, we do no longer find that every chakra corresponds to a advantageous emotion or mental state. Rather, every petal of every lotus chakra corresponds to a definitely one in every of a type intellectual or emotional usa, and there seems to be no fashion through which we can also need to create a sign for the chakra as an entire.

That's not all, despite the truth that. There isn't always any foundation in Indian sources for the numerous connections made in Anodea Judith's Wheels of Life. According to Judith, every chakra corresponds to a one in all a kind gland, set of symptoms and signs and symptoms and signs and symptoms, set of components, metal, mineral, herb, planet, yoga posture, tarot match, sephira, and archangel in Jewish and Christian mysticism, respectively. These correlations do now not appear within the number one literature. Judith or her educators probably made them up based completely mostly on a few shared traits. According to high-quality books and net web sites, this also applies to the essential oils and crystals that art work with every chakra. (It's definitely genuinely worth noting that Judith does include a few material from an particular Sanskrit deliver [namely the aa-cakra-nirpaa, for which see below] below the term "Lotus Symbols" for every chakra.)

Not that envisioning a selected crystal cleaning your manipura chakra by using using placing it on your stomach whilst feeling low in self-esteem is a lousy idea. Perhaps; it simply depends on who you ask. While my approach is unconventional and has no longer been attempted and actual during generations (it truly is, in the end, the aspect of way of life), I firmly consider that there may be extra to life than what I can fathom with my limited, rational thoughts. However, I expect it's far crucial for the general public to apprehend while a method's lineage only goes once more some a long time in place of centuries. No want to manufacture origins if the method works, proper?

2. The chakra structures are normative as opposed to descriptive.

This is probably the most critical interest. In English, the chakra tool is normally supplied as a reality of existence, with many descriptive languages (like, "the muladhara chakra is at the lowest of the backbone, and it's miles red," and so on.). Even even though maximum historic Sanskrit texts do no longer offer us with information approximately the arena as it's far, they do offer us with a particular yogic exercising: we're to think about a subtle item at a particular factor in the body, long-installed like a lotus or a spinning wheel, made of colored mild, after which prompt mantric syllables in it, for a particular reason. This will let you honestly apprehend my preliminary assertion. The books prescribe movement, outlining the stairs one need to take to perform a purpose by manner of magical approach. Sanskrit is written in an elliptical form, so while it says a few element like "4-petaled crimson lotus at the lowest of the frame," we are predicted to take it as due to this, "The yog need to keep in mind a four-petaled lotus..." For in addition clarification, please check with object #5 under.

three. The chakras and the highbrow conditions they constitute are very well present day and western.

The muladhara chakra is associated with protection and survival, the manipura chakra to the power of man or woman and a wholesome feel of self confidence, and so on, as stated on innumerable internet websites and in limitless courses. The well-knowledgeable yogi may be conscious that linking chakras to emotional or intellectual states is a mainly modern improvement that can be traced lower again to Western psychologist Carl Jung. Possibly for some people (although usually now not with out priming), such institutions represent real reports. We do not find them within the

Sanskrit resources. I'm conscious that the high-quality real exception is the ten-chakra device for yogi-musicians, which I've written about on my blog. However, within the system superior spherical 1300 CE, we do not locate that each chakra corresponds to a selected emotion or mental nation. Rather, each petal of each lotus chakra corresponds to a exclusive emotional or mental united states of america, and there appears to be no pattern with the useful resource of which we can also need to create a label for the chakra as a whole.

The story does not surrender there, despite the fact that. Almost not one of the connections made in Anodea Judith's Wheels of Life can be traced lower lower back to particular Indian texts. Judith tells us that every chakra corresponds to a completely unique gland, contamination, meals, metallic, mineral, herb, planet, yoga posture, tarot card healthful, Jewish mystical sephira, and Christian archangel.

The assets provide no evidence for those correlations. Judith or her educators possibly made them up considering that they seemed much like actual human beings. This additionally applies to the crucial oils and crystals that, in line with certain books and internet web sites, are related to every chakra. (It is in reality honestly well worth noting that Judith does encompass some cloth from the original Sanskrit supply [that is, the a-cakra-nirpaa, for which see below] below the term "Lotus Symbols" for each chakra.

However, this doesn't advise that putting a selected stone on the belly at the same time as struggling with low arrogance and visualizing the crystal cleansing of the manipura chakra will assist. Perhaps so, albeit it's miles predicated upon on the reader. Though this method has no longer been carried out for generations, I firmly be given as actual with there's a high-quality deal extra to existence than what I can fathom with my gift diploma of rationalism. But I suppose it's far essential for the general public to be aware at the same time as a exercising most effective has a few a long term of facts within the lower back of it in region of centuries. If a technique works, there need to be no need to lie approximately in which it got here from, right?

Hey there—do you want to have a look at extra

four. Contrary to commonplace belief, the seven-chakra machine was no longer derived from an historical textual content however as an opportunity a dissertation penned in 1577

The Western yoga community generally adheres to the chakra machine as "overdue and truly unorthodox" in a previous draft of my journey. A few days later, I understood that I had been misinformed; the rad-tilaka, a submit-scriptural document from the thirteenth century, offers a more simplified version of the equal seven-chakra device. However, the rad-tilaka clarifies that there are numerous chakra structures (alongside side structures of 12 or 16 chakras). A more sure implementation of this tool is decided within the 'iva-samhit,' which dates decrease again to the 14th or fifteenth century. Yet, the majority of yogis (each Indian and Western) are acquainted with the seven-chakra gadget manner to Prnanda's art work from the 16th century, or as an alternative, way to the fantastically incoherent and careworn translation of it finished with the beneficial resource of John Woodroffe in 1918.

Nonetheless, it's miles correct to nation that the seven-chakra system has ruled the Western world for the past four or 5 centuries. However, the Western seven-chakra tool you are familiar with modified into superior from the misinterpretation of a non-biblical deliver via manner of occultists in the early 20th century. This in no way disproves it but highlights its dominance problems.

five. A chakra system's primary responsibility is to characteristic a blueprint for nysa, the location of mantras and deities.

The unique authors believed that the primary characteristic of the chakra tool become to feature a blueprint for nysa, which refers to the place of mantras and deity energies at strategic places throughout the diffused body. As a result, despite the fact that loads of masses of people are inquisitive about chakras, every so often any are sincerely using them in any inexperienced way. It's all proper if it is the case. I haven't any goal of proving anybody incorrect; as an opportunity, I choice to tell those seemingly. These 3 elements of the particular chakra structures stand out due to the fact the maximum exceptional: Each chakra is associated with a specific Great

Element (Earth, Water, Fire, Wind, and Space), and each Great detail is associated with a one of a kind Hindu deity. As I referred to, that is because of the reality the chakra gadget serves typically as a model for nysa. The exercising of nysa (from the Sanskrit word for "place") is mentally "placing" a mantric syllable in a specific chakra of the power body and silently intoning its sound.

The exercising is rooted in a cultural placing in which the Sanskrit language's sounds are seemed as incredibly effective vibrations that may feature an efficient element of a magical exercise to accumulate emancipation on a spiritual or cloth diploma through magical way. Although the workout of Western yogis may also moreover in no way be as important as it's miles for someone who grew up with those deities as paradigmatic icons etched on their unconscious brains, invoking the photograph and electricity of a given deity into a specific chakra is also culturally specific.

Every chakra has a huge presence of the so-known as Cause-deities (karana-devats). Ganesh, Brahma, Vishnu, Rudra, vara, Saddiva, and Bhairava form a real collection, with the primary and last deities not continuously performing depending on the form of chakras. Since the remaining deity of any unique faith is enthroned inside the sahasra or thousand-petaled lotus at the crown of the top (technically no longer a chakra, thinking about Kualin pierces chakras in her climb or fall), the god at the prevent of the list of Cause-deities is in no way that deity. Since the Goddess is the ideally fitted god in lots of those systems, Bhairava (Shiva's most esoteric form) is satisfactory included in the listing of Cause-deities even as the Goddess transcends him.

6. The substances put in every chakra decide which seed mantras are suitable for use with that chakra.

It's not as complex because it sounds. You have heard that the muladharachakra's seed mantra (bija) is LAM. But unluckily, it's far no longer. Furthermore, VAM isn't always the svadhisthana chakra mantra. Whoa, maintain on a 2nd. That's because of the reality the solution is easy: In maximum chakra visualization sports, the muladhara is programmed with the Earth element seed-mantra LAM (rhymes with 'thumb'). As the Water element's seed mantra, VAM is rooted in swadhisthana (at least, within the seven-chakra tool you recognise about). In the equal manner, the phrase RAM represents the detail of fireplace, YAM is the detail of wind, and HAM is the place of vicinity. (All those bijas bring about 'thumb,' despite the fact that I need to factor you that in esoteric Tantrik Yoga, the essential bijas produce other vowel sounds which may be taken into consideration a long way stronger.)

The critical mantras listed underneath the primary five chakras on every page you could find out on Google do now not belong to the chakras themselves however as an opportunity to the 5 pre-installed elements. You'll need this facts if you ever skip the region of one of the additives. To which the speaker responds, "Gasp! I can do this?" Totally. The Elements are set up in quite severa locations in the course of Tantrik traditions. For example, the earth is located on the center of one's being in the Saiddhntika lifestyle. What do you decided ought to probable take place in your relationships while you usually positioned the Wind detail in the middle of the coronary heart? (Remember that O.M. Is the inherent mantra of the anahata chakra and that YAM is the chant of Air/Wind.) Have you observed that current American yogis have quite tumultuous romantic partnerships? Do common invocations of wind at the level of the coronary heart have a few aspect to do with this? Nahhh….

(Since just a fraction of my audience has gotten this a long manner, I could have sufficient money to be humorous.) Since grounding blessings cardiovascular health, you could want to bear in mind putting in some Earth within the coronary heart ultimately. Knowing that LAM is the mantra for the Earth detail in place of the muladhara chakra is useful in this example.

Additionally, the bulk of the present day geometric figures used to represent the chakras can extra as it should be be located below the elegance of the Elements. Earth is typically fireside with the aid of manner of a downward-pointing (crimson) triangle, depicted via manner of a (yellow) square, Water by means of a (silvery) crescent moon, space with the aid of way of a circle, and wind via way of a hexagram or six-pointed movie star. You now comprehend that the geometric shapes related to every chakra are symbols representing the

Elements in preference to capabilities of the chakras themselves.

Finally, even a Sanskrit supply may be misunderstood, which brings me to my very last argument. For instance, the 5 Elements are placed in the first five chakras of a seven-chakra tool. However, in all of the classical systems, the Space element is placed on the crown of the cranium, in which the yogi reports an wonderful beginning into countless spaciousness. Since vicinity is the only trouble that vanishes certainly into infinity, it glaringly belongs on the top. It turned into exposed to a Kaula lifestyle wherein the classical Cause-deities had been driven all the way right down to make room for later, better deities (like Bhairava and the Goddess), and the elements were saved tightly sure to the deities and chakras with out plenty room for trade. This is a style that has unfortunately continued. (Despite this, it isn't proper now clean that the concept have become drawing on Kaula assets, as he does now not enthrone the Goddess at the sahasrara, as one may want to anticipate in a Kaula seven-chakra system, but alternatively Paramaiva, perhaps due to the have an effect on of Vedanta.

We have slightly began to find out this issue depend. I am no longer making this up. Looking into the academic literature, collectively with that of Dory Heilijgers-Seelen and Gudrun Bühnemann, will display you actually how complicated this mission rely is. To have a look at such paintings, now not to say create it, requires unusual hobby and staying electricity. That being stated, proper proper here's what I'm hoping comes of this entire located up: a little modesty. A little fewer claims to authority close to pretty esoteric matters. There is probably a reduction within the extensive form of yoga instructors who need to provide an explanation for the chakra device to their college college college students.

Even after fourteen years of reading Sanskrit, I locate the number one assets daunting.

Most of this place has no longer however been explored. Don't, consequently, assert information inside the area of chakras. Please inform your yoga college students that there's simplest one example of the chakras in all the books they will study. Almost now not whatever published in English may be considered definitive for yoga practitioners. So, on the same time as you are nonetheless learning, why now not maintain your yoga beliefs more gently? Let's be sincere about how little we comprehend about those historic yoga practices. Instead of trying to skip yourself off as an professional on a watered-down version of them, you must inspire your college students and your self to take a deeper, more introspective look inside. After all, your yoga exercise includes all information and attention from each yoga draw near at some point of statistics.

The purpose of Chakras

1. Root Chakra (Muladhara Chakra)

As the idea chakra, Muladhara is wherein we discover balance. When someone's equilibrium is off, they may revel in feelings of being unanchored, risky, disturbing, afraid, and indignant due to a lack of energy and course. Positive emotions like stability, self warranty, stability, strength, independence, and power update the ones poor ones while the muse chakra is in concord.

Purpose: Financial Independence, Survival, Security, Stability, Self-self notion

Position: At the lowest of the backbone, near the tailbone (between the anus & the genitals)

Maturity age: 1-7 years

Stone: Hematite

Element: Earth

Color: Red

Yoga fashion: Vrkshasana (Tree Pose), Virabhadrasana (Warrior Pose), Ardha Setu Bandhasana (Half Bridge Pose), Tadasana (Mountain Pose), Shavasana (Corpse Pose)

2. Sacral Chakra (Swadishthana Chakra)

This chakra enlightens us about our emotional connections with others and ourselves. The sacral chakra likewise manages power and creativity related to sexuality. When the Sacral chakra is blocked, a person reviews anger, dissatisfaction, and emotional explosiveness. Feels uninterested in energy and concept; may be manipulative or preoccupied with sexual fantasies. When this chakra is in harmony, you enjoy an growth in optimism, pleasure, strength, compassion, instinct, and contentment.

Purpose: Pleasure, sexuality, feelings, creativity, preference, and procreation

Position: Lower stomach (2-four hands underneath the navel)

Maturity age: eight-14 years antique

Stone: Amber, Tiger's eye, opal, topaz

Element: Water

Color: Orange

Yoga fashion: Trikonasana (Triangle Pose), Kakasana (Crow Pose), Baddha Konasana (Bound Angle Pose)

3. Solar Plexus Chakra (Manipura Chakra)

This chakra is related to one's feeling of self, enjoy of manipulate over one's existence, experience of community, and functionality to define and articulate one's values. If you may think about a time while you felt anxious or aggravating, that became the Manipura Chakra reaction. Extreme self-doubt and guilt upward thrust up while the Solar Plexus chakra is obstructed. When this chakra is in harmony, we are able to specific ourselves authentically. We have greater strength, experience extra ordinary in our abilities, and interest extra on achieving our desires.

Purpose: Self-esteem, life reputation, will, strength, self-self perception, strength, movement, and satisfaction

Position: Solar plexus, higher stomach, among lowest ribs and navel

Maturity age: 15-21 years antique

Stones: Yellow stones (Amber, Calcite, Citrine, Quartz, and Topaz)

Element: Fire

Color: Yellow

Yoga style: Paschimottanasana (Classical Forward Bend), Dhanurasana (Bow Pose), and Bhujangasana (Classical Cobra Pose).

4. Heart Chakra (Anahata Chakra)

This chakra connects the materialistic lower chakras to the spiritual better chakras (related to spirituality). When out of whack, the Anahata Chakra can result in terrible feelings, which incorporates wrath, mistrust, tension, jealousy, irritability, and worry. As one's emotional and intellectual health decorate, one turns into extra empathetic, beneficial, wonderful, social, and pushed.

Purpose: Love, compassion, understanding, take delivery of as real with, forgiveness, generosity, and receptivity to others are all essential trends for this characteristic.

Position: At the coronary coronary heart's plexus (Heart)

Maturity age: 21-28 years vintage

Stone: Rose Quartz

Element: Air

Color: Green or pink

Yoga style: Ushtrasana (Camel Pose), Ardha Setubandhasana (Half Bridge Pose), and Matsyasana (Fish Pose).

5. Throat Chakra (Vishuddha Chakra)

The Anahata chakra is primarily based at the Vishuddha chakra to have a voice and preserve its strength in communication. When the throat chakra is blocked, we grow to be introverted and not able to talk our minds. When the Throat Chakra is in concord, we are able to speak our minds, communicate efficiently, be innovative, and experience happiness.

Position: Depth of the throat, connecting with the thyroid gland

Purpose: Self-expression, Communication, and reality

Maturity age: 29-35 years antique

Stone: All blue stones Aquamarine, sodalite, chalcedon, lapis lazuli

Element: Music and Sound

Color: Turquoise and Light Blue

Yoga fashion: Matsyasana (Fish Pose), Sarvangasana (Shoulderstand), and Halasana (Plough Pose)

6. Third Eye Chakra (Ajna Chakra)

The Third Eye Chakra (Ajna Chakra) is a place of attention and popularity cultivated thru asana exercise. Ascending the torso brings us inside the route of union with the divine. It has been said that clearing the Ajna chakra through meditation brings approximately freedom and intuitive notion acquired in preceding lives.

It is characterized through intelligence, belief, self-knowledge, and intuition. When out of whack, you could enjoy symptoms together with inclined aspect, loss of self assurance, and a worry of fulfillment, as well as modifications in your character (inclusive of extended narcissism) and physical health (along with migraines, blurred vision, seizures, and spinal dysfunctions). One's shallowness and power increase whilst Ajna's chakra is healthful and functioning (spiritually and emotionally).

Purpose: Imagination, instinct, liberation, foresight, clairvoyance, and thoughts

Position: The place within the middle of the forehead, above the zero.33 eye

Maturity age: 36-forty years vintage

Stones: Amethyst, sapphire, fluorite, labradorite, opal, moldavite, zircon

Element: Light

Color: Indigo or pink

Yoga fashion: Balasana (Child's Pose), Shirshasana (Headstand)

7. Crown Chakra (Sahastrara Chakra)

The crown of the top homes the Sahastrara Chakra, the 7th and very last chakra inside the human electricity tool. Spirituality, lively concept, energy, know-how, and cosmic cognizance originate within the 7th chakra. If the Sahastrara chakra is blocked or imbalanced, it could result in horrific emotions and persistent infection and sorrow.

Purpose: Spirituality, frequently taking place or natural focus, and enlightenment

Position: Above the pinnacle

Maturity age: 40 3-forty 9 years antique

Color: White, Deep Purple

Element: Divine Consciousness

Stones: Diamond, hyaline quartz

Yoga Posture: Shirshasana (Headstand)

Chapter 7: The Seven Foremost Chakras

These strength hubs are known as chakras. They run along the spine within the astral frame, from the tailbone to the top of the cranium. Our physical body houses an electricity body referred to as the astral body. There is a heavenly counterpart to each part of the bodily body. Your astral body is invisible and untouchable. Additionally, this is why our eyes are not able to come upon the chakras.

Each of the seven chakras gives out a splendid hue and outstanding of energy. Each one corresponds to a particular gland within the frame. It is notion that blockage or ailment of a chakra can cause physical, mental, or emotional illnesses due to the truth each chakra is associated with a super hassle of our being. Wellness and health give up end result from interest to and concord among those strength factors.

Root Chakra

The perineum, the lowest of the backbone, is the bodily area of the premise chakra. The first energy center in your frame is your root chakra. It's getting access to the basics like meals and water, a constant vicinity to stay, and a network to experience such as you belong. It binds us to the earth, our loved ones, and ourselves. Root chakra-related verbs are "I actually have" and "I am."

Color: The root chakra is associated with pink due to the fact it's far linked to the circulatory system, which incorporates blood and oxygen. The root chakra is related to crimson due to the fact it is a very primitive hue.

Causes of Blockage Feelings of anxiety and residing thru extended stress can cause a blocked root chakra because of the reality it's far engaged in our combat-or-flight reaction (strain reaction). Pain within the bones or joints is a symptom of an obstruction in the frame's energy drift, at the side of emotions of anxiety, uncertainty, and separation.

In all its manifestations, self-care is crucial for restoring chakra stability and organising the muse chakra. Red factors like beets can be restoration for the basis chakra, as can earthy food like potatoes and carrots, which give extra grounding energy. The root chakra additionally may be activated through manner of eating distinctly spiced meals and meat, which can be exquisite protein belongings.

Sacral Chakra

The sacral chakra represents transformation and versatility in contrast to the concept chakra's balance. It's a symbol of imagination, feeling, and sexuality. The sacral chakra, decided within the decrease belly, is associated with sexuality, fertility, and creativity. A verb meaning "I experience" quality describes the sacral chakra.

Color: Orange is a stimulating and creative shade associated with the sacral chakra. Since the sacral chakra governs our creativeness, sensations, and sexuality, orange stimulates the ones regions on the same time as additionally bringing consolation and pride.

Symptoms of a blocked sacral chakra embody a loss of creativity, inflexibility, impotence, and problems with the reproductive organs (uterus, bladder, and kidneys). Emotional distress and the disability or unwillingness to take part in exciting or sexual activities are extra possible effects. The sacral chakra can be realigned and opened via project sports activities that supply you pleasure and foster your modern talents, in addition to through going for walks in the direction of elegance of alternate and the matters over that you haven't any energy. Foods like tangerines, oranges, almonds, and loads of water can assist nourish the sacral chakra.

Solar Plexus Chakra

The sun plexus chakra, determined within the higher stomach, actually under the rib cage, is the seat of private power and self-guarantee. It's the stuff of transformation and the source of our hearth, energy, and pride. Use the affirmations "I can" and "I do" to stimulate your solar plexus chakra and fill yourself with self belief if you revel in willing.

Color: Yellow is the shade of the sun plexus chakra. The shade yellow is related to bravery, friendliness, and stimulation.

The solar plexus chakra is the seat of private electricity and aspiration. Hence its blockage can result in feelings of confinement, weak point, powerlessness, vulnerability, digestive problems, and infection or fury. Faith in oneself and one's instinct is important for restoring chakra stability and beginning the solar plexus. Yellow substances, together with corn, grain, and teas like peppermint and chamomile, can help stability your sun plexus chakra.

Heart Chakra

After our physical and emotional desires were addressed, we're free to love surely. The heart chakra begins offevolved at the chest and travels down the fingers and into the palms. Affinity, oneness, restoration, equilibrium, connections, and compassion are all associated with the coronary coronary heart chakra. The verb "I love" is associated with the coronary coronary heart chakra.

Color: Although we extra commonly be part of the coronary coronary heart with red or pink, inexperienced and purple are actually related to the coronary coronary coronary heart chakra. The coloration green has lengthy been associated with a feel of fitness and power and progressed recognition and compassion.

Symptoms of a blocked coronary heart chakra encompass emotions of hatred, retreat, judgment, cardiovascular contamination, bronchial allergies, and compromised immunity. If an crucial connection fails, you can suffer envy, rage, and suspicion, all of which might be signs and symptoms and signs and symptoms of a blockage.

To repair concord and release blockages inside the coronary heart chakra, popularity on loving and being concerned movements within the course of oneself and others. Leafy greens, herbs, and green tea are all inexperienced food which can be suitable for the coronary coronary coronary heart chakra.

Throat Chakra

This chakra, placed in the location throughout the throat, is associated with the capacity to particular oneself and to talk mind and feelings to others in addition to to as a minimum one's very own thoughts and body. The throat chakra hyperlinks our vocal cords with our capacity to talk verbally, musically, creatively, and authentically. The topics that provide us pleasure echo at the same time as our throat chakra is balanced. The verb "I talk" corresponds with the throat chakra.

Color: Turquoise and Light Blue are the coloration. The blue hue, related to the thoughts, is concept to stimulate the throat chakra. This chakra is connected with the shade blue, which stands for cause, verbal exchange, and trustworthiness.

The disability to explicit oneself, a lack of hobby in looking after oneself, thyroid troubles, the commonplace cold, and a loss of notion in a single's private and expert lifestyles are all signs and symptoms of a blocked throat chakra. You apprehend the sensation if you've ever been too concerned or guarded to open up to a few different man or woman.

By prioritizing truthful expression and powerful use of electricity, you can restore concord and open the throat chakra. One dependable manner to maintain your throat chakra clean is to talk up for your self and others. All forestall result, juices, and beverages can advantage the throat chakra.

Third Eye Chakra

One's 0.33 eye chakra is the seat of 1's intuitive colleges and visible, imaginitive, and clairvoyant counterparts. This chakra, positioned proper within the middle of the forehead, is symbolic of our transcendental popularity. Insight, hobby, and illumination all originate within the 1/3 eye chakra. The verb great describes the 1/three eye chakra is "I see."

Color: Indigo, an intermediate color among blue and purple, is the hue most commonly related with the 1/3 eye chakra. The hue indigo has a calming, reflective, and intuitive impact on its website online traffic.

If your 1/3 eye chakra isn't functioning, you may revel in highbrow strain or stubbornness similarly to disorientation, complications, and eyestrain. A blockage in the 0.33 eye chakra can ward off your desire-making, mainly about your interests and desires, as it's far engaged to your instinct and your capability to faucet into not unusual feel and reasoning.

The zero.33 eye chakra can be realigned and unblocked via "preserving off illusion" or going decrease lower back to attempted-and-real strategies. Purple additives, together with blueberries, grapes, and plums, further to chocolate and lavender-flavored drinks or spices, can be beneficial for the third eye chakra.

Crown Chakra

The crown chakra, similar to the premise chakra, connects us to the universe and the cosmos. The crown chakra, which sits on the pinnacle of the top, is attached to enlightenment, spirituality, meditation, and higher states of awareness. The crown chakra is the seat of bliss and enlightenment, in which we are able to in the end see things as they may be. Crown chakra verbs encompass "I understand" and "I understand."

Color: For the crown chakra, rich red and white are recommended. As a photo of concord and religious enlightenment, the violet conveys a enjoy of improvement and openness to new tales.

Apathy, a loss of connection to the religious global, and psychological issues that make it difficult to research and communicate are all signs of a blocked crown chakra. When the crown chakra turns into unbalanced, reconnecting with nature and our "better being" through sports activities like workout and deep breathing outside within the sunshine are pinnacle priorities for restoring harmony. Since a healthful crown chakra implies healthful energy pathways at a few level inside the frame, no specific meals are perception to restore the crown chakra.

How well do the 7 Chakras relate to every one of a kind?

To be honestly healthful, you want to be aware of and strike a balance amongst seven exquisite components of your health. Is it a twist of destiny that seven power facilities inside the frame, or chakras, need to be balanced and open for maximum top notch functioning? The harmony of our seven chakras is critical to our intellectual, emotional, and non secular well-being.

Preventing chakras from becoming susceptible or obstructed is extra vital than preventing them from becoming "too robust." It's critical to strike a balance considering the fact that simply as little of a few thing can be terrible, so can an excessive amount of of some problem else. IIN's fitness training program is based totally on a seven-dimensional version that considers all additives of health.

Chapter 8: Balancing And Recuperation Your Chakras

Do you sense "off" as of overdue? Do you regularly make insignificant mistakes on the undertaking? Have you been sick for additonal than consistent with week now? You may be experiencing an imbalance in your chakra device if you're going through the ones tough times, and there are numerous feasible reasons. Chakras—what are they?

When your chakras are not in concord, how do you comprehend? Chakras are factors of reputation for the frame's crucial power. Although there can be loads of chakras, maximum humans best pay attention to the seven vital ones. The sushumna nadi, the body's middle channel, is aligned with these surprising power wheels.

The location wherein the left channel (ida nadi) and the proper channel (pingala nadi) meet is where the sushumna nadi's chakras keep splendid sway. The time period "subtle frame" describes this community of electricity pathways and mental hubs. Though it exists out of doors of the geographical regions of the physical body and the mind, the diffused body considerably impacts all of these components.

When all of the body's electricity facilities (chakras) are unblocked and prana (life stress) can flow freely among them (via the nadis), the human organism thrives. Instability and disharmony can be delivered on thru the usage of whatever that disrupts or damages the frame, thoughts, or soul. The goal is to reap concord. If you feel out of sorts, you may start to discern out what is incorrect through focusing in your chakras.

If you are feeling off-kilter, it can be due to a number of of factors, together with what you've been ingesting (food, drink, mind, reviews), in that you're in existence proper now (visiting, moving, large transitions), and the time of three hundred and sixty five days (wind, cold, rain, warmness, dryness). All of these have the functionality to have a large impact on your sensitive human frame.

Chakras are important to provide an explanation for the human gadget in the philosophies of yoga and Ayurveda, which maintain that "like will increase like" and "opposites balance." This approach that you can experience even more warm temperature and agitation than regular if you're already experiencing some form of excess warmth on your body (along with rage or indigestion) and then upload greater warmness (which include a warmth day or mainly spiced meals).

If you are taking a chilly bathe or consume a few fresh fruit, however, you may revel in higher and additional in balance because you are together with the alternative to the equation. An professional in power remedy and the writer of Anatomy of the Spirit. Your biography will become your biology with every idea and experience.

www.ingramcontent.com/pod-product-compliance
Lightning Source LLC
Chambersburg PA
CBHW071440080526
44587CB00014B/1925